Alga

Brian & Eileen Anderson

Published by
Landmark Publishing
12 Compton, Ashbourne
Derbyshire DE6 1DA

Edinburgh
Dublin
London
Berlin
Paris
Barcelona
Rome
Lisbon
Madrid
ALGARVE
Faro

N
W E
S

ALGARVE

Opposite page: Mértola, walled town

Algarve

Brian & Eileen Anderson

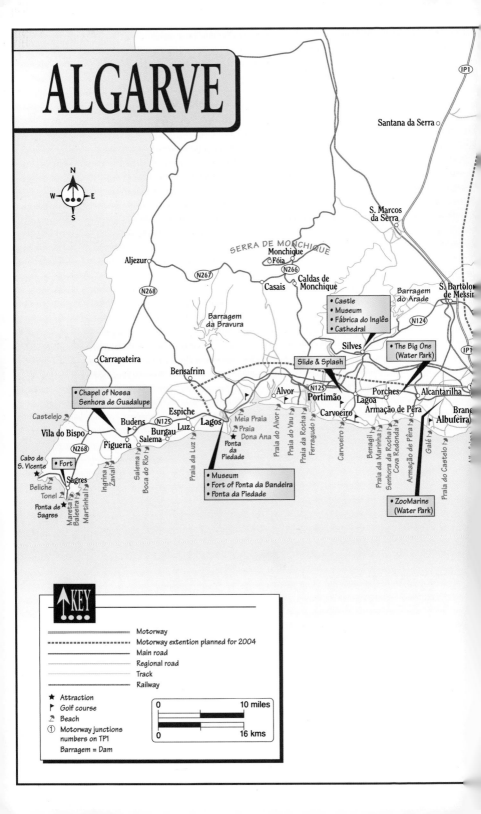

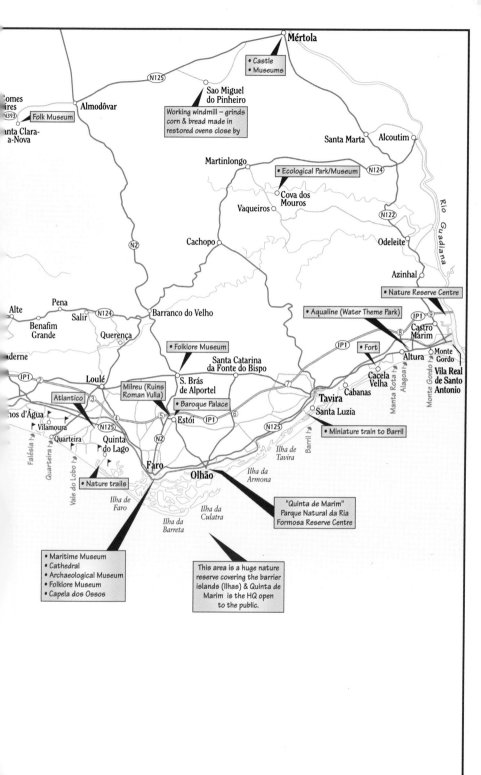

CONTENTS

• Feature Boxes •

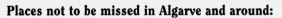

Places not to be missed in Algarve and around:

Silves: lovely Moorish town on the riverside with a castle, cathedral and a lively cultural centre based around an old cork factory.

Sagres: wonderful atmosphere at the wild and westerly tip of Algarve. Watch the locals defying death to fish from impossible ledges on the high cliffs.

Monchique and Fóia: the high mountain village of Monchique is the gateway to Fóia, the highest peak in Algarve, which offers, on a good day, the best view in the region.

Estói: watch out for its monthly market, which is the most famous in Algarve, with a brisk trade in animals and a show ring for riders. A good sized area of Roman remains (*Milreu*) and the intriguing Estói Palace gardens are also worth a visit.

Mértola: although just outside Algarve in neighbouring Alentejo, the historic walled town of Mértola is one of the most beautiful in the country. There is a castle to see and a number of small but interesting museums.

Portimão: this is not the prettiest of Algarve's towns but good for shopping and the place to eat freshly caught sardines by the riverside.

Ponte da Piedade, Lagos: by the lighthouse here is some of the most wonderfully sculptured coastline. Rock stacks, arches and grottoes create powerful images certain to keep the camera clicking.

Faro old town: atmospheric walled nucleus of modern day Faro, inside which is the cathedral and interesting archaeological museum housed in a sixteenth-century convent.

S. Lourenço: an exquisite example of an 'Azulejos' decorated church interior.

Cova dos Mouros: an ancient copper mine now museum. Experience Algarve's wilder interior and visit some remote villages.

Faro Marina

Introduction

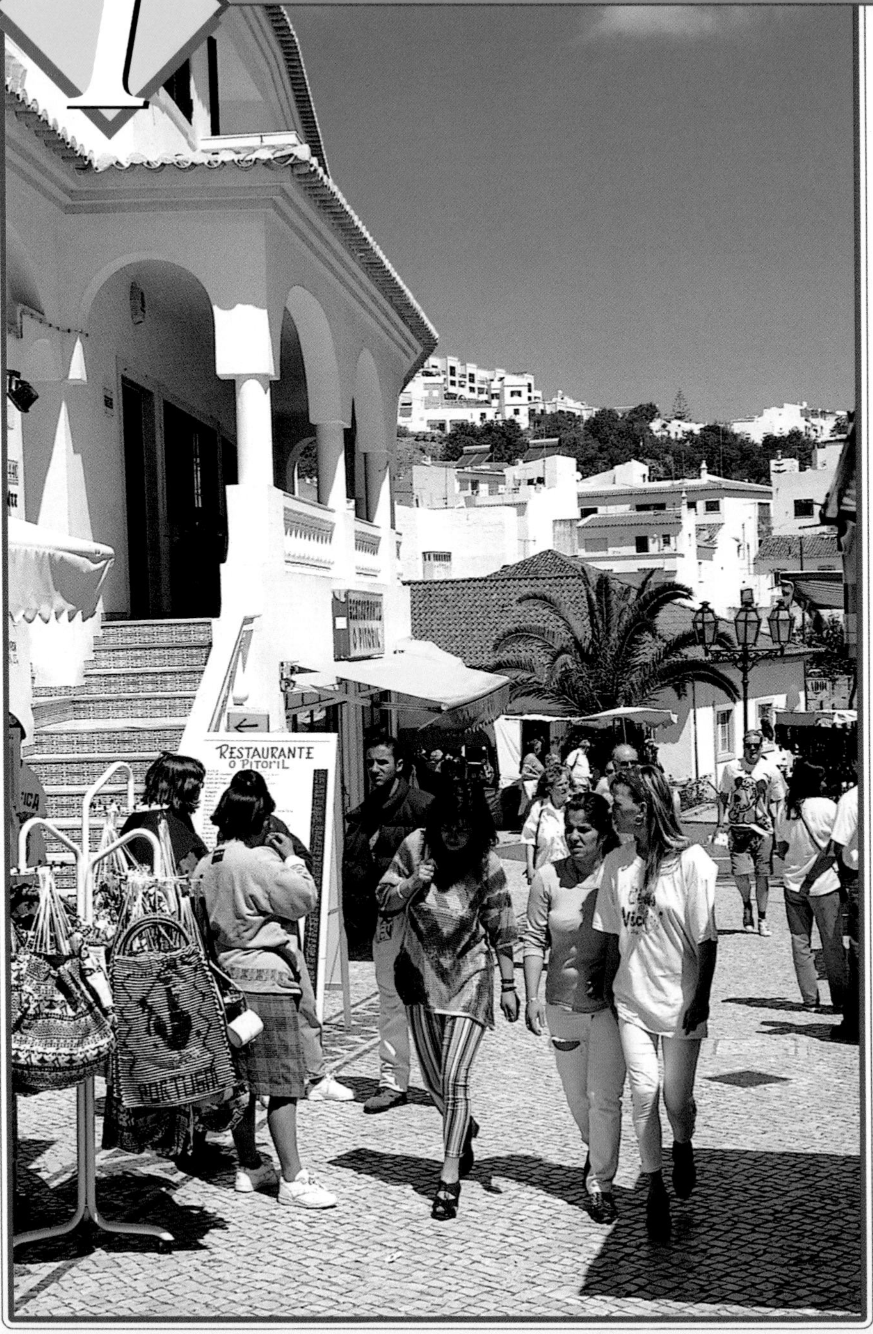

I f sun and fun on Europe's finest beaches is high on the holiday agenda, then Algarve is the right choice. It is the right choice too if the opportunity for some gentle excursions to explore the countryside and the culture of this most southern part of Portugal is part of your holiday formula. For the lively and active looking to expend some energy, Algarve boasts a wide range of sporting facilities from horse riding, tennis, walking, watersports and especially golf. New golf courses seem to sprout up every year and there are never enough. Many of the courses are carefully crafted around weather cut coastal cliffs to offer scenery so spectacular they could easily bring new converts to the game!

Algarve has been entertaining tourists for a good number of years and is, in many senses, a maturing destination. This brings advantages with well developed services and amenities but it does not mean that the whole region is crowded out with hotels and developments. In recent years, some new hotels have been springing up in the interior, which make ideal bases for countryside enthusiasts.

The region still offers a good mixture of lively, built-up resorts like Albufeira, quieter resorts like Luz, undeveloped coastline where coastal walks are still possible, plenty of quiet countryside and old villages to explore and even some fairly high mountains. Those on the culture trail will not be disappointed and can pick their way through the ruins left by the Romans, the Visigoths and the Moors. Whatever makes up the perfect holiday, Algarve has it and from the agenda laid out in this Landmark guide, you can pick and choose your way to a perfect holiday.

LOCATION AND LANDFORM

Algarve occupies a relatively narrow strip of land running east to west across the most southern part of Portugal. It is separated from neighbouring Alentejo in the north by a low range of sparsely populated hills and from Spain in the east by the River Guadiana, while a restless Atlantic forms the southern and western boundaries. The province is not especially large, just about 100 miles (160km) from east to west and roughly 20-25 miles deep (30-40km).

Across the central region, from the coast inwards, is a fertile lens-shaped region of limestone known as the Barrocal. Here the rich terra-rosa soil supports endless orchards of oranges, almonds, figs, olives and vines and is often described as the garden of Algarve. There is a distinct change of land use to the north of the Barrocal. The low, straggling mountains, the serras, stretching east to west are composed of acid schist which yield extremely poor, stony soils of low fertility sustaining little in the way of agriculture. Much of the highly undulating landscape in this under populated area is covered with the drab-looking sticky-leaved *Cistus ladanifer*. Just looking at a map of Algarve, the distribution and density of villages in the central region virtually marks out the fertile area of the Barrocal.

The Serra de Monchique is different again. It is largely composed of a particularly attractive form of blue granite that is extensively quarried in the area. It enjoys the highest rainfall in the region and soil depths are sufficient to allow the mountain pastures to be farmed. It lays claim to the highest peak in Algarve, at Fóia, near Monchique, which ascends to a height of 2960ft (902m). With a paved road running all the way to the summit, it has become something of a tourist attraction.

THE PEOPLE

The Portuguese are not as outgoing as some Mediterranean people, like the Greeks for example, and they have a touch of the English reserve about them. This is all very superficial and it takes little to break through to find that they are truly friendly people. Friendliness has its boundaries though and it takes a long time to build up a relationship that leads to an invitation home.

It is a Catholic country and deeply religious but this is far less evident in Algarve, although churches are still well attended and most cultural activities and festivals have strong religious connections. There is nothing more important to them than the family and this remains a strong institution. Children are generally adored in Portugal and they often get more attention in restaurants and similar places than their parents.

ART AND CULTURE

The most expressive form of art in Algarve is seen in pottery. There are shops and factories the length of the province, each one selling a selection of usually brightly coloured, sometimes hand painted, pots or plates. As in other Mediterranean cultures, traditional pottery must serve the

Azulejos

One particular speciality of Portugal is seen in painted tiles, known as *azulejos*, which has been an art form in Portugal since the sixteenth century when the Italian majolica technique was introduced. In this process the tile was covered with a white enamel so that it could be painted. Early tiles concentrated on geometric designs and tapestry patterns but styles and techniques developed slowly throughout the seventeenth century and other motifs appeared in the art work including animals, fish and flowers in a range of exotic colours. The polychrome fashion waned with the introduc-

dual function of both being useful and decorative.

FOOD AND DRINK

The Portuguese are hearty eaters and love their food. Typical Portuguese restaurants are mostly found now in country areas since the main resorts and towns have taken on a more international flavour. Most of these restaurants still offer a menu that balances Portuguese and international dishes. A wide selection of other cuisines is represented, Indian, Chinese, British, and others. Pizza places abound, largely because the Portuguese themselves love them. Vegetarians too are catered for and there are a number of specialised eating places to be found in the more popular areas.

tion of Delft blue. The delicate blue and white tiles that it produced rapidly found favour in Portugal.

By the eighteenth century, narrative tiles had appeared, which depicted events in life or history like harvesting grapes or hunting, and they grew bigger in scale to cover large walls. They became popular for decorating churches with religious scenes, public buildings and eventually even the outer walls of private houses. There are many examples to be seen in everyday life and they are often used to make up street names in Algarve. Porches Pottery will paint an *azulejos* panel to order in any design required, possibly from a photograph.

Pre-dinner nibbles

The moment diners sit down at a table, some starters in the form of bread, butter and olives are placed on the table and these are normally included in the cover charge. Sometimes cheese, ham or paté are also placed on the table but, beware, these items will appear separately on the bill. If not required, ask for their removal straight away to avoid a charge.

On the menu

The menu usually lists fish and meat dishes in equal numbers. There are few surprises amongst the meat dishes. Pork, steak, chicken (*frango*) and turkey (*peru*) are all popular but watch out for the hot and spicy chicken piri-piri, very popular with the Portuguese. Kid (*cabrito*) too is a local favourite and is sometimes served in slices like roast meat but more often cooked in a casserole.

Sardines are universally enjoyed here, especially for the lunch time trade, and they are often cooked on charcoal grills in the street outside the restaurant. The smell of grilling sardines can be quite tempting, particularly between June and September when sardines are in season and likely to be fresh. Traditionally they are served with boiled potatoes but there is often an option of chips in tourist areas.

Most fish on the menu will be fairly familiar including salmon (*salmão*), red mullet (*salmonete*),

Continued on page 14...

11

Above: Olhos d'Agua
Below: Albufeira

Right: Algarvian cart used for decoration

Below: Santa Luzia

sole (*linguado*), mackerel (*carapau*), plaice (*solha*), bream (*pargo*), tuna (*atum*) and hake (*pescada*) but there are also many other species of fish caught in the Mediterranean waters which are totally unfamiliar and sometimes turn up on menus. Fish is expensive in restaurants and often priced per kilo, which makes it look astronomically expensive. The nor-mal procedure is for the restaurant to weigh the chosen fish and charge accordingly, sometimes the waiter will advise the weight before cooking but, as a rough guide, an average serving is around 400g. *Bacalhau*, dried, salted cod, is something of a national dish and appears on many menus.

Bacalhau

L ooking like off-white smelly cardboard and sold in every super market, *bacalhau*, dried cod fish, is a speciality dish dearly loved by the Portuguese but treated with the utmost suspicion by everybody else.

One boast is that there are at least 365 recipes for preparing *bacalhau*, so it can be served in a different way every day of the year. All the recipes start by soaking the *bacalhau* in water to reconstitute the fish and remove the salt, after that it is cooked in various ways and often topped with a sauce. One of the more popular recipes, *Bacalhau à Bras*, is cooked with onions and eggs and served with thinly sliced potatoes. When *bacalhau* is properly soaked and desalted, it can be good, otherwise it is not but this is down to individual taste. The only advice is to try it and see.

Sausages (*chouriço*)

Morning coffee with a tasty cake is a national pastime in Portugal. No matter where it is bought, the coffee is always excellent, which is perhaps not too surprising for a country which once ranked some of the great coffee producing countries, like Brazil, Angola and Timor, amongst its colonies.

Coffee is served in a bewildering variety of ways. The Portuguese mainly prefer a *bica*, a small strong coffee, which is good for a quick fix of caffeine but hardly slakes a thirst. Worse still, the small cup is only half full so for a full cup ask for a *cheio* which simply means full. Milk lovers can ask for a *pingo* which will bring a small strong coffee with a drop (*pingo*) of milk but for a larger coffee ask for a *meia de leite* which is usually a normal cup size, half of strong coffee filled up with hot frothed up milk.

In areas like Algarve, *café com leite* is well understood and it usually produces a white coffee but if less milk is preferred then '*só pouco leite*' added to the order should result in a less milky coffee. To be sure to get a large cup add the word '*grande*'. Two more coffees which are invariably on the list are *galão*, weak, milky coffee served in a glass and *galão direita* which is half milk, half coffee served in a glass.

Few coffee shops sell coffee without selling cakes (*bolos*) which look like, and taste like, home-made confectionery although they may be on the sweet side. Some parts of the country have their own specialities but not Algarve. Rice cakes (*arroz*) offer a light sponge which is not usually so sweet, *bolo da rocha* is a delicious bun with a coconut top and filled with custard whilst coconut cakes, *cocos*, are also good. Doughnuts are mostly filled with custard but for something plainer try the *palmier* which look like butterfly wings.

The Cataplana

Introduced by the Arabs, *cataplana* dishes are particularly popular in Algarve. A *cataplana* is a hinged metal pan, traditionally with a long handle so it can be pushed into the fire. It has a heavy, close fitting lid, and behaves a little like a pressure cooker. *Cataplana* dishes appearing on the menu usually involve sea food, especially clams, but meat dishes with pork are occasionally offered. Usually the *cataplana* is brought to the table so that diners can enjoy the rich aroma released when it is opened.

Desserts (*Sobremesa*)

There is not usually much of a choice in most Portuguese restaurants.

Crème caramel or pudim flan and *arroz doce*, a sweet cold rice pudding, are universally popular and appear on most menus but there is always the choice of ice cream or fresh fruit.

From the wine list

Almost every region of Portugal produces wine, which leads to a vast array of labels and makes choosing even more difficult. Terms to look out for on the label are *Garrafeira* which means that it has been aged in the cask for at least two years followed by a year in the bottle and *Reservas* which are selected wines and spend even longer in the barrel. The following summary lists only the major regions or types:

Vinho Verde: the vines for these wines are grown in the north of the country and typically up trees or over pergolas. They are light, around nine per cent in alcohol, crisp, slightly acid and gently sparkling wines which go well with chicken or salads and are particularly refreshing in hot weather. Vinho Verdes are often listed separately on the wine list, look for Ponte de Lima wines that are amongst the best. Other wines are listed under Vinhos maduras.

Douro wines: these are grown and made along the river Douro, in the same region as the port wine grapes. There are some exciting red wines to be found under this label which includes Barca Velha, acknowledged as the countries best wine and made only in limited quantity.

Dão wines: grown in central Portugal around Viseu, live on a good reputation but are losing out now to other regions, particularly to Alentejo. Generally, the region produces good full-bodied reds but look out for Grão Vasco in both red and white.

Barraida: This is produced in the region just north of Coimbra and is best known for its reds. Look out for the garrafeiras and usually the older the better.

Setúbal: this is a fairly small wine growing area just south of Lisbon but it produces some good wines including Periquita, a full-bodied red wine made by Fonseca. Especially worth trying is the aromatic dessert wine Moscatel de Setúbal, also made by Fonseca, which manages to combine the flavour and richness of the muscatel grape without the cloying effect often produced in sweet wines.

Alentejo: this region has improved its wine quality significantly in recent years through investment in new equipment and technology. It is producing many good and inexpensive wines that are well worth trying. These include Reguengos, Redondo and Vidigueira, both red and white.

Algarve: local wines are not the best to be found in Portugal but the wine from Lagoa is worth a try.

Port Wines: Portugal is the home of port wine and there are a good many famous labels. For something a little different, try chilled white port as an apéritif.

CLIMATE

Although not strictly in the Mediterranean, Algarve does enjoy a Mediterranean climate of hot dry summers and mild wet winters. As always, there are variations within any type of climate and this is true in Algarve.

Summers generally are the most reliable season with almost continual sunshine and very little rainfall. As a consequence of its position on the

Atlantic, the intense heat of summer is pleasantly tempered by cool westerly winds. These breezes are not necessarily uniform across the province but tend to be most strongly felt in the west, roughly from Albufeira westwards, and can be particularly fierce on the promontories of Sagres and Cape St Vincent. For this reason the western part of the province is termed the Barlavento (windward) and the eastern side the Sotovento (leeward) and these terms are in common use, sometimes being used to replace east and west

If there is a rainy season, it is between October and March, but many winters turn out to be very dry. Winters are generally mild and, with the sun shining, it is perfectly possible to spend days on the beach basking in the sun, especially since many beaches are backed by high cliffs to the north making them effective sun traps. Evenings and early mornings can be chilly enough to pull on a warm jumper but light clothing is all that is needed for the hottest part of the day.

Spring, March through until May, is one of the loveliest seasons with the countryside decked in flowers. Temperatures are on the rise and by April most tourists are out and about in shorts.

WHEN TO GO.

Algarve has a climate that encourages tourism all year round. Obviously, the peak period is in the main summer months of July and August when there is an influx of tourists from many countries in Europe as well as from Spain and Portugal itself. Facilities can get stretched in this busy period, popular beaches crowded and it may be necessary to queue for a preferred restaurant. The whole place buzzes and life, in places, pays no attention to the clock, either day or night.

Winter holidays

Winter is a more relaxed time in the tourist industry but the region does entertain a lot of visitors on long stay holidays. There is a tendency to group these in popular locations like Albufeira, Lagos, Praia de Rocha and Monte Gordo in the east. Concentrating the visitors in this way means that more restaurants and other services are prepared to stay open to offer a wider selection.

Given good weather, winter can be a delightful time to explore the region. It is not difficult to get around, the inland villages seem at their most natural, the display of almond blossom for which Algarve is famous peaks in January and February, the orange and lemon trees are laden with fruit and the pace of life is relaxingly slow. Only the golfers seem active. It is possible to play golf in Algarve throughout the year but the winter months are by far the most popular.

Spring is an irresistible season anywhere and this is doubly true in Algarve. Judging by the flowers,

Continued on page 20...

The Portuguese calendar has its fair share of red letter days; public holidays, Saints days and festivals. Banks, post offices and government offices are closed on national and local public holidays. Restaurants and some shops normally stay open. Public transport is often interrupted too, reverting to either a Sunday service or none at all. Many smaller petrol stations also close but larger ones, especially along main routes, remain open. It pays to ensure a full tank of petrol 'just in case' at these times. Christmas Day is an exception though, when nearly everything is closed except for a selection of restaurants that advertise the fact they are open well in advance. The days to watch out for are:

1 January	New Year's Day
March/April	Shrove Tuesday (Carnival), – Good Friday
25 April	Liberation Day (for 1974 revolution)
1 May	Labour Day
May/June	Corpus Christi
10 June	Camões Day
15 August	Feast of the Assumption
5 October	Republic Day
1 November	All Saints Day
1 December	Independence Day (from Spain in 1640)
8 December	Immaculate Conception
25 December	Christmas Day

There are plenty of celebrations throughout Algarve at the time of public holidays with Loulé sporting the largest and liveliest Carnival before the start of Lent and São Brás de Alportel a celebration with flowers on Easter Sunday. Alte, starting mid afternoon, is the main venue for folk dancing on 1 May. Collect a leaflet, produced monthly, from Turismo, which details local events.

Fairs and festivals are paramount to the Portuguese who throw themselves wholeheartedly into their celebration. The Algarvians may not be as religious as their northern compatriots but religion is nevertheless an important element in their lives. Many festivals have religious connections, often stemming from earlier pagan rituals, but once the festivities have been blessed in church the locals certainly know how to have a good time. Events in the larger towns and villages have become more geared to tourism, so for a more authentic atmosphere head out to villages in the countryside.

Of the religious festivals, Easter is the most important. Carnival actually begins during the month before Lent and represents a final excess of enjoyment before the more sober weeks of Lent. It is also a celebration of the end of winter, which implies the incorporation of pagan rites into Christianity. Lent culminates with a sombre Good Friday and processions enacting the burial of Christ, particularly at Faro, Lagoa, Olhão, Tavira and Vila Real, before a joyous return to things normal on Easter Sunday.

Loulé's patron saint, Nossa Senhora da Piedade, has been the focus of Algarve's most important pilgrimage (*romaria*) of the Mãe Soberana (Sovereign Mother) for more than four hundred years. On Easter Sunday, the statue is transported, with little ceremony, from its sixteenth-century chapel on a hill overlooking the town to the church of St Francis in Loulé. Full pomp and ceremony though are attached to the procession that returns the statue to its sanctuary two weeks later.

Festivals, including those of a more secular nature, sprinkle the calendar of Algarve.

January	International Almond Blossom Cross-Country Race
February	National Orange Festival at Silves
April/May/June	Algarve International Music Festival
May 1	Alte Festival in celebration of water
July	Silves Beer Festival
July	Feira do Carmo at Faro (Agricultural Fair/Crafts)
August	Sardine & Seafood Festival at Olhão
September	Algarve Folk Music & Dance Festival finals at Praia da Rocha
October	International Algarve Car Rally
October	Algarve International Dog Show
Christmas	Christmas remains a religious celebration for the Portuguese and relatively low-key compared with other parts of Europe.

spring starts around March and stretches through April into May. The tourist industry moves up a gear and many places, like the water theme parks, start to open their doors with the greater influx of visitors. Sunbathers will no doubt find it warmer on the beaches but the Atlantic is still cold for swimmers. With the spring flowers bursting into bloom, the countryside is at its greenest and most colourful. This is the best season for walkers and lovers of the countryside and, with the weather not too hot, it is good too for those participating in sports.

Early September is still peak season in Algarve and tourist numbers remain high throughout the month. Tourism starts to decline only in October although this is still a very popular month with many searching for the last drop of summer. Most facilities stay open well into November, and possibly into December, whilst there are sufficient numbers around but the whole metabolism of the region slowly declines back towards the gentler pace of winter.

NATURAL ENVIRONMENT

Flora

Algarve is blessed with a profusion of wild flowers that are seen mostly throughout the early spring months. Flowers occur throughout the province. Sagres and the central Barrocal limestone region are particularly rich in species and the latter is especially good for wild orchids. From March to May tireless enthusiasts might be able to find as many as twenty different species, including a selection of bee orchids, like the amazing mirror orchid, *Ophrys vernixia*, which has a deep blue mirror-like speculum.

Narcissus lovers will delight in finding the paper white narcissus, *N. papyraceus*, which is fairly widespread and usually found in damp locations, the diminutive *N. gaditanus* and the cheerful *N. bulbocodium* but all these are early flowering species, especially the paper white. One of the brightest yellow flowers is the *Anemone palmata* that is seen here and there, as is *Tulipa australis*. The wild *Paeonia broteroi* grows throughout the region

Fruit growing is an important industry, particularly citrus fruits, peaches and almonds, in Algarve and these provide spectacular blossom displays in spring. Almond blossom, often called the snow of Algarve, turns the fields white in January and February and the air is heady with the smell of orange blossom in April.

Fauna

Most of the animals in Algarve have either been eliminated or reduced to low levels by the activities of the hunters. Rabbit, fox and genet are amongst the survivors and, perhaps more surprisingly, so is the wild boar. Their digging marks can often be seen in country areas and even on golf courses, which makes them extremely unpopular with the golfing fraternity. Lizards abound with the Moorish gecko prominent around coastal areas, particular on or near walls. Snakes are around too although the one most commonly encountered is the harmless grass snake, but care should always be exercised since there is a species of viper around although rarely seen. Algarve is pure heaven for bird

Top: Oranges,
a major crop
in Algarve

Above left: One
of the author's
relaxing in a
poppy field

Above right:
Narcissus
papyraceus

Right: Cistus
crispus

spotters with something in the region of 300 or so species seen throughout the year. With all the river estuaries, marshes and old salt flats, there are a good number of areas where birds can easily and regularly be seen. Many of these areas are protected as reserves, like those at Castro Marim, the Rio Formosa Natural Park and the Quinta do Lago reserve which is part of the Rio Formosa Natural Park but on a different site.

HISTORY

Portugal came together as a nation only in 1297 with the Treaty of Alcanices that was signed after Algarve was liberated from the Moors. Prior to this, the history of Algarve followed a different course, which was less violent and traumatic than that of the north.

In around 700-600BC, the north was invaded by the warrior-like Celts but few filtered down south and there is little evidence to suggest that they colonised Algarve. Peaceful Phoenician traders from the eastern Mediterranean were around about this period and they settled in Algarve to form trading colonies, which they established throughout the Mediterranean, They searched inland for metals and built up a trade in tin, copper and salted fish. Greek traders had joined them by the sixth century BC but Carthage was on the rise and the Carthaginians were soon to eclipse the Phoenicians. They stayed until their war with Rome.

Under the Romans

As a result of the Second Punic War (218-212BC), the peninsula as a whole passed to the control of the Romans and Portugal was simply part of Hispania Ulterior. The Romans met little trouble in colonising the southern coastal region but had much more difficulty conquering the interior. By the fifth century, waves of barbarians, the Vandals, the Alani and the Suevi, swept over the Pyrenees and down over Spain and Portugal bringing Roman domination to a close.

The 400 years of Roman rule may be long forgotten but they left a legacy of the Romance language, the legal system, roads and bridges. They introduced agricultural practices including irrigation and are credited with introducing the grape vine. There are some tangible remains to see in Algarve, like the garum tanks where a fish paste was made for export and the remains of one or two villas, particularly at Milreu near Estói.

Early in the sixth century, the Visigoths started to establish a somewhat tenuous rule over most of the peninsula which they held until the arrival of the Moors early in the eighth century.

The Moors

The arrival in the south, in 711, of the Moors from Africa seriously challenged the Visigoth rule. They overran Spain quickly and moved steadily northwards into Portugal pushing Christianity north of the Douro, an area that was never really conquered by the Muslims. The South of Portugal became part of Spain and was known by the Moors as Al-Garb (the West) evolving eventually to the modern name of Algarve. They established a capital at Shelb, now Silves, and set about ruling with a great deal of tolerance, respecting the rights of the Christians and the Jews to practise their own religions.

Social order brought considerable advances with the Moors allowing smallholders to rent land owned by the state, encouraging work to improve irrigation techniques introduced by the Romans and moves to introduce new crops including oranges, lemons and cotton. Centuries of harmony gradually decayed with the decentralisation of rule and with the arrival at the end of the eleventh century of more militant Muslim groups like the Almoravid.

The emergence of a nation

Battles to remove the Moors started in the north immediately they arrived and the first victory for the Christians was at the Battle of Covadonga in the Asturias in 718. Slowly and painfully the Moors were pushed back south but it was many centuries before Algarve was recovered.

In 1189, Afonso Henriques' successor, Dom Sancho I, used the help of passing crusaders to make a determined attack on western Algarve. He succeeded in capturing Silves against massive odds but was only able to hold it until the following year. The Moors swept back to take control of much of the southern region in what proved to be their last great campaign. Dom Sancho II and his successor, Dom Afonso III continually pressed the Moors until they were finally ousted from the territory in 1249 and Christianity was fully restored.

Resisting the Castilians

Castilian resentment at the emergence of Portugal as a nation was put aside in 1297 with the signing of the Treaty of Alcanices. This formally recognised the definitive borders of Portugal. Protecting the new borders was uppermost in the thoughts of Dom Dinis (1279-1325) who set about building or restoring castles with enormous energy.

Castle building

Whole lines of castles were built to protect either the borders or possible invasion routes. These defences were enlarged and improved by successive kings right through into the eighteenth century leaving the country now with a remarkable heritage of fine military architecture. Algarve has only a few; there is a castle at Silves, ruins at Paderne and a castle and a fort at Castro Marim against the border with Spain.

Fear of Castilian domination was never far from the surface. There were continual inter-marriages between the royal and noble families to feed the ambitions of the Castilians whilst still maintaining Portuguese independence. It almost proved to be the downfall of the country when the first dynasty, the House of Burgundy, came to an end with no heir to the throne.

Juan of Castile laid claim to the Portuguese throne under the terms of the marriage contract to Leonor of Portugal. He was widely supported by Portuguese nobility but fiercely rejected by the people. João, an illegitimate son of Dom Pedro and Grand Master of the Order of Avis, came forward with popular support

Above: Cacela Velha

Left: Mayday celebration at Alte

Below: Fishermans beach at Armação de Pêra

to claim the crown. This led to the Battle of Aljubarrota (1385) in which João, backed by a force of English archers, roundly defeated superior Castilian forces to become Dom João I, the first king in the House of Avis. In recognition of English support, relations with England were sealed through the Treaty of Windsor in 1386 and, in the following year, the marriage of João to Philippa of Lancaster, daughter of John of Gaunt.

The Age of Discovery

Dom João I and Philippa raised some brilliant children including Pedro, who travelled widely sending home maps and works of geography, and Henry the Navigator. Henry played a very significant early role in the discoveries and founded a school of navigation at Sagres in Algarve, using his power and wealth to staff it with the cream of Europe's cartographers, astronomers and navigators. During his lifetime Madeira (1419), the Azores (1427) and the Cape Verde Islands (1457) were all discovered and colonised and the west coast of Africa explored.

Opening new trade routes brought with it enormous wealth and not just in gold. Spices from the East, cinnamon, cloves and peppers, grain, sugar and dyestuffs from Morocco and slaves from Africa, activated the merchants and stimulated the development of key overseas trading posts,

not always achieved without battles. On a more humble scale, one product from their discovery of Newfoundland, *bacalhau* (dried, salted cod) became virtually part of the staple diet and remains so even today. This period of Portugal's history produced some epic heroes, a stable economy but no lasting wealth. Only the monarchy, taking a royal fifth from all trade revenues, benefited but even its wealth had no permanency.

An Age of Decline

Dom Manuel (1495-1521) was quite an enlightened king who established royal authority and introduced many beneficial reforms, which were continued by his successor, João II. Literature was flowing from the printing presses and the humanistic influences of Europe were making a noticeable impression. Colleges were established and the university at Lisbon was moved permanently to Coimbra in 1537.

Permitting the establishment of the Inquisition as a tool of the monarchy was a turning point that led Portugal into decline. Slowly and steadily the Inquisition became a reign of terror and a whole entrepreneurial class was snuffed out, robbing the country of the engine to drive the huge commercial empire it had striven so hard to build.

Stability still held with the ascension of the young Dom Sebastião in 1557 but strains in the economy were showing which became overpowering around the 1570s when increasing competition, falling prices, foreign debts and a drop in productivity signalled a serious decline.

Sebastião, an unstable and idealistic king, yearned for a crusade against the Moors in North Africa and when he sensed the time was right he emptied his coffers to equip an 18,000 strong force. It sailed to Morocco from Algarve in 1578 but met a superior force at Alcacer-Quiber and was effectively annihilated. Around 8,000 were left dead on the battle field including the king and many young nobles with the rest helplessly taken prisoner, a 100 or so escaped capture. The modernistic statue of Sebastião in Lagos, looking more like a biker than a warrior, never fails to attract attention.

Cardinal Henrique, an elderly uncle, assumed control and further weakened the country by paying ruinous ransoms for the release of prisoners. He died after only two years in power leaving no male heirs. King Philip II of Spain invaded and was installed as King Filipe I of Portugal in 1581.

The Castilian Usurpers

Although this rule was initially unpopular, the union with Spain brought short term advantages to the economy. Spanish wheat helped to feed the people and Spanish soldiers helped to guard the Portuguese empire. Filipe started well by observing Portuguese autonomy and leaving control of the Cortes and the judicial system entirely with the Portuguese while promising that the Portuguese language would remain and that their empire overseas would still be ruled by Portugal.

Apart from the first two years, the whole of the Castilian reign was conducted from Spain. After sixty years, Spanish domination came to an end in 1640 with a popular uprising against Filipe III on 1 December. This day is still remembered as a national holiday.

The House of Bragança

The Duke of Bragança was crowned João IV in 1640 and with Spain seriously distracted on other fronts, there was no immediate opposition. Dom João focused his efforts on rebuilding the country, placing its independence beyond doubt and gaining recognition abroad. England agreed to renew the old alliance of 1386 and treaties were signed with Charles I (1642) and Oliver Cromwell (1654). Later, in 1661, the alliance was strengthened by the marriage of Charles II to Catherine of Bragança. Although skirmishes with Spain waxed and waned, and taxes rose to fairly high levels, it was a quietly successful reign which had also seen the emphasis in trade swing from India to Brazil.

Towards the end of the seventeenth century, economic problems were looming with the loss of maritime trade to other nations but the discovery of Brazilian gold was to change that, at least for a time. Under Dom João V, Crown revenues soared and the money was spent on building palaces, churches and monasteries but the heavy expenditure almost bankrupted the state.

José, Dom João's successor, was genial and easy going. He shared his father's love of the arts, particularly opera, and was happy to leave the affairs of state in the capable hands of his minister, the Marquês de Pombal. Pombal was to go down in history as one of Portugal's greatest statesmen, admired by some but reviled and hated by others. His was an oppressive dictatorial rule exercised by using the royal prerogative rather than his own personal power.

Natural disaster

It was church as usual for the people of Lisbon on All Saints day, 1st November 1755, when a terrifying and furious earthquake suddenly hit the town. Buildings collapsed everywhere and fires from the many church candles added further devastation. After nine days of raging fires the heart of the city was reduced to ashes. Much of the surrounding country was also seriously affected as shock waves spread as far as Algarve to the south yet the north of the country escaped serious damage.

Left: Monte Gordo   Right: Decorative pottery

27

The Jesuits laid the blame for this divine retribution entirely on Pombal. After surviving an assassination attempt, Pombal declared the Jesuits and certain nobles as responsible and took his revenge with executions and by disbanding the Jesuit movement in 1759. Granted emergency powers by the king Pombal set about rebuilding Lisbon in a simple grid fashion with houses of a neo-classical style.

Oppressive though his regime was, his policies helped to reform Portugal's economy and lay the foundation of the modern Portuguese state. Towards the end of King José's life, Pombal plotted to force Maria to renounce her rights to the throne for her son, José, who was a disciple of Pombal. It failed and, on her succession, Maria tried Pombal for crimes against the state and confined him to his estates.

One of the difficult to reach coves, near Praia da Marinha

Enter Napoleon.

In 1807 Napoleon delivered an ultimatum that Portugal declare war on Britain and close its ports to British shipping. Since Portugal was dependent for half her trade on Britain and on British sea power to protect her trade routes, there was little option but to reject Napoleon and face the inevitable war.

The monarchy immediately slipped off to Brazil to set up court there as the French, under General Junot, entered Lisbon. The Portuguese invoked the alliance with Britain and an expeditionary force commanded by the brilliant tactician, Sir Arthur Wellesley (later the Duke of Wellington) quickly defeated the French. In all there were three waves of French attacks in the Peninsula War, all repelled, but it left the country fatally weakened. The French failed to pay the agreed compensation and another Anglo-Portuguese treaty, this one in 1810, gave Britain the right to trade freely with Brazil eliminating Portugal's lucrative middleman's role. Brazil itself was proclaimed a kingdom in 1815.

Towards democracy

A new constitution was adopted in 1822 which assured the establishment of broad voting rights, no special prerogatives for nobles and clergy, a liberal Cortes more truly representing the people and the end of the Inquisition. These additional freedoms brought dissent, the formation of political parties and constitutional wrangles, which continued for the next thirty years. Things did not get better with Portugal steadily losing control of its colonies, allowing its rate of development to fall behind that of Europe and, towards the end of the nineteenth century, witnessing the growth of the Republicans.

Portugal's last king, Manuel II ascended the throne in 1908. His attempts to appease the Republicans also proved futile and the monarchy was violently overthrown on 5 October 1910. Dom Manuel, the Unfortunate, went into exile in England where he died in 1932.

The Republic.

It can hardly be said that the Republicans grasped their opportunity with both hands. It is true that they won an overwhelming victory in 1911 with strong support from the urban and rural poor but they promptly disenfranchised much of their support by introducing electoral laws based on literacy. Unrealistically high hopes of the Republican supporters never materialised. There were further measures which alienated support, like the Law of Separation, passed by parliament in an attempt to divide the church from the state and gain control of the Catholic church. Weak economic factors, cyclical revival of the monarchists and general political turmoil brought about forty-five changes of government in the years up to 1926.

Dictatorship

The Democratic party was overthrown in a bloodless coup on 28 May 1926 and the military took control. António de Oliveira Salazar, a well known professor of economics, was asked to take the post of finance minister but he resigned soon afterwards on the grounds that he did not have sufficient power. The country's finances declined still further and, by 1933, Salazar was reinstated with greater powers. Slowly but surely, he assumed the role of dictator and kept the country under tight control, almost as a police state, until a deck chair accident in 1968 followed by a stroke led to the end of his career.

Back to Democracy

There was no easy path back to democracy. The instability following the death of Salazar seemed to be resolved by a bloodless military coup on 25 April 1974 and the formation of a Junta of National Salvation. Elections were organised but they failed to bring political stability, with a constantly changing government, sixteen in the space of the four years up to 1978. Political instability continued for the next decade but Mário Soares managed to win popular support as prime minister on three occasions. He emerged with enough support to become the first civilian head of state in sixty years.

In 1986 Portugal entered the European Community which initiated changes greater than at any time in the past. Funds poured in to help modernise the infrastructure and, with increased foreign investment, the country enjoyed a sustained period of economic growth. There is a new wealth about with many now enjoying a good standard of living but it masks a deep poverty still experienced in parts of the countryside.

From large to small, from lively to quiet, Algarve has sufficient variety to suit all tastes. In general terms, the largest concentration of tourists and some of the bigger resorts lie between Faro and Praia da Rocha, next to Portimão. East and west of the central coastal area, tourist numbers reduce and resort sizes decline quite dramatically.

The following gives a thumb nail sketch of the main resorts to help in making the most suitable choice. For more details see the main section and the Good Beach Guide.

EAST TO WEST:

Monte Gordo

Monte Gordo: the nucleus of the old fishing village is still there but now swamped by big hotel developments. This resort has the advantage of being set on level ground with easy access to the massive, sandy beach. A beach side casino livens up the night life and there is plenty of choice bars and eating places.

Manta Rota (Altura)

Manta Rota (Altura): small but developing steadily, particularly at Altura; oceans of sand.

Tavira

Tavira: an attractive town set in the river mouth but with limited accommodation. The nearest beach is on the Ilha de Tavira, a short ferry ride away.

Faro

Faro: this is the capital of the region and little used as a resort. The nearest beaches are near the airport out on Ilha de Faro, which can be reached by a bridge although there is a ferry service from Faro.

Quinta do Lago and Vale do Lobo

Quinta do Lago and Vale do Lobo: both of these are exclusive resorts developed by big international companies. They are a mix of luxury accommodation and golf courses set in 2,000 acres (800 hectares) of pine forests on the edge of the Rio Formosa Natural Reserve.

Quarteira

Quarteira: pretty is the last word to spring to mind. The drab huddle of high density concrete tower blocks which greets visitors on entering the resort must sink a few hearts but the ambience improves a little when the promenade is reached.

Vilamoura

Vilamoura: this is another privately developed resort covering a massive 4,000 acres (1600 hectares). Attractively laid out with plenty of green lawns and verges, it includes a busy marina and yet more golf courses. It is a place for doing rather than seeing although there is plenty of beach space for relaxing.

Olhos d'Água

Olhos d'Água: tucked down at the bottom of a narrow cleft, this small fishing village is full of character and the sea front is as pretty as any in Algarve. Much of the accommodation lies at the top of the hill. Overlooked by most large tour operators, it still gets crowded in summer.

Praia da Oura

Praia da Oura: on the fringes of Albufeira. Once a charming cove, Praia da Oura has yielded totally to the developers. Bars, shops and restaurants crowd the narrow one-way road, known as The Strip (streep), which leads down to the cove, and apartments are everywhere else. In summer it is taken over by the young and lively which usually means drugs and trouble these days. Something of its old charm is restored out of season when things quieten down. A good but small beach.

Albufeira

Albufeira: once a small fishing village this is now the most densely developed and popular resort in Algarve. Originally situated at the bottom of a large natural amphitheatre, white buildings now cover the whole of the enclosing hillsides. It is big, it is lively with plenty of amenities and has an attractive beach which gets covered wall to wall with bodies in high season. Being almost centrally situated, it makes a convenient base from which to explore the whole of the province. The outskirts, around Montechoro for example, make a particularly accessible base from which to explore the countryside, especially outside the main season.

Galé

Galé: another small resort now developing rapidly into villa land. No need to fight for beach space here.

Armação de Pêra

Armação de Pêra: yet another disaster of concrete tower blocks but, once beyond, the promenade is very attractive with a fine beach and the old heart of the town is interesting.

Carvoeira

Carvoeira: it is hard to imagine the days when this was just a small sandy cove used by the fishermen. Massive development spreading up the hills on both sides has completely swamped the resort providing far too many bodies for the size of the beach.

Praia da Rocha

Praia da Rocha: an attractive promenade and plenty of beach but it has also suffered from over development. Some of the accommodation is so far from the front that there may be a long walk in store unless hotel transport is available. Plenty of night life and restaurants but mainly towards the promenade area.

Vau

Vau: a smaller resort on the periphery of Praia da Rocha. It has a beach large enough to take a lot of bodies without becoming crowded. Expect it to be on the quieter side.

Alvor

Alvor: this is an attractive old village located on a hill by the river estuary whilst the resort accommodation is developing at the seaside just under a mile away.

Lagos

Lagos: spread along the riverside, elegant and lively Lagos is one of the most attractive resorts in Algarve. It has no immediate beach, which may have saved it from the worst excesses of the developers but a ferry takes bathers to the superb Meia Praia just across the river. Closer to hand, there are a number of small sandy coves along the coast out to Ponta da Piedade.

Luz

Luz: a small fishing village with a good beach but expanding. Quiet with good walking opportunities along coastal cliffs.

Burgau

Burgau: tiny fishing village full of character tucked into a narrow crevice. Beach opportunities limited.

Salema

Salema: the most westerly of Algarve's resorts, Salema is again an expanding fishing village but it remains relatively uncommercialised. Fairly quiet and with plenty of beach space.

Relaxing by the sea, Albufeira

Algarve boasts the finest collection of beaches anywhere in Europe. Some are in the most spectacular settings enclosed by sculptured cliffs, others are long and flat but they share one thing in common, tons and tons of fine golden sand.

There is a marked difference between the beaches in the east and the west. East of Quarteira, the beaches tend to be more extensive, forming long strands running for miles, and are easily accessed without the need to descend steps. Huge sandbars, known as *Ilhas* or barrier islands, surround the coastline at Faro creating a lagoon full of mud banks and channels that can clearly be seen from the air when flying into Faro airport. This enclosed area is protected as the Ria Formosa Natural Park. Many of these barrier islands can be reached by ferry from the nearby coast and offer a particular advantage. The Atlantic has days when rollers stream in with such ferocity that it is dangerous for all but the most experienced swimmers to bathe or even paddle. Then, these sand banks may offer an inward, protected beach where the sea is calm and the waters warmer.

West of Quarteira, starting at Falésia, the cliffs rise and stay at a high level for much of the remaining coastline, relenting in only a few places. This may mean that there is a steep flight of steps to tackle to reach the sand, not so convenient with young children and lots of gear to carry. It probably also means that the beach is a sun trap with little shade since the whole of this section of the coastline is south facing and the cliffs rise behind the beaches to the north. It is these cliffs, often strikingly hued, which give the beaches in the west so much appeal. They have been cut and shaped by the elements carving out coves of

Safe Bathing

Most beaches in Algarve operate a warning system of flags to indicate sea bathing conditions.

Red flag; danger, the water is off limits.

Yellow flag: paddling at the water's edge is safe but the sea is off limits to all except strong swimmers.

Green flag; generally safe for all swimmers.

Chequered flag: there is no guard on duty.

great character often leaving rock stacks either offshore or on the beach and even rock arches in places.

There are also acres of undeveloped empty beaches on the west facing coast of Algarve but the Atlantic is distinctly more energetic here with breakers constantly rolling which are good to see but dangerous for bathing. None of these is included here.

There are more than sixty named beaches but the selection listed includes only those around major resorts and some of the more isolated spectacular beaches worth the trouble to visit even if it means walking. A sign '*Praia*' pointing off somewhere should lead to a beach. Remember too that the sea here is not the Mediterranean but the tidal Atlantic Ocean and many beaches lose area at high tide. The beaches are listed east to west:

BEACHES EAST OF FARO:

Monte Gordo

Monte Gordo: level access to a deep stretch of fine sand. Can walk for miles since it extends virtually all the way to Cabanas near Tavira. Sun beds and shades are available and there are plenty of refreshment facilities close to hand.

Ilha de Tavira

Ilha de Tavira: one of the huge sand bars which can be reached by ferry from Tavira, by a miniature railway from Pedras d'el Rei or by foot following the path alongside the railway. It is good for wind surfers and the facilities available include refreshments, sun beds and shades.

Ilha de Faro

Ilha de Faro: a summer settlement runs down the middle of this sand bar. Can be reached by ferry from Faro in the summer months or by car along the airport road. With its close proximity to Faro, it does get crowded in summer but there are plenty of facilities on hand.

BEACHES WEST OF FARO:

Falésia: attractive with its multitinted cliffs. Some seventy-five steps lead down from a small car park and café to a large stretch of sandy beach with plenty of space for those determined to get away from the crowds. Some limited facilities in the way of sun loungers and shades.

Olhos d' Água

Olhos d' Água: very beautiful beach full of character with attractive, enclosing cliffs and rock stacks on the sands; eastern part shared by fishermen. Steep downhill approach, limited parking with cars restricted during the main season but easy access to the sand by a short flight of steps or ramp.

Santa Eulalia

Santa Eulalia: not on many maps but follow signs found between Balaia and Oura. This is a pretty beach of good size and fine sand backed by cliffs and umbrella pines. Access is good, free of steps, and facilities close to hand.

Praia da Oura

Praia da Oura: The Strip winds down to a small, enclosed bay with good facilities; gets very crowded in season.

Albufeira

Albufeira: picturesque beach lent considerable character by the enclosing cliffs and by the occasional rock stack. Sun loungers and shades are available. There is easy access at the eastern end from where fishermen operate but otherwise there are steps to cope with. Although this is a long stretch of beach, it is hard to see the sand for reclining bodies in high season.

Praia do Castelo

Praia do Castelo: there is a parking area for this popular beach which lies some distance from any real density of tourist accommodation. Some forty-eight steps lead down from the cliffs to this fairly large

Above: Galé; sandy cover
Left: Galé; sculptured cliffs
Below: Olhos d'Agua

cove which is flanked by additional coves. There is a restaurant/café at beach level and lounging facilities as well as a beach shower.

Galé

Galé: this beach serves the small but expanding resort area of Vale de Parra. The cliffs descend more or less to sea level from Galé westwards to Armação de Pêra leaving something of an interest mix at Galé itself. To the east there are all sorts of little coves amongst the highly eroded low cliffs, all connected by a footpath that weaves behind. To the west there is a large stretch of sand backed by sand dunes and pines which stretches all the way to Armação de Pêra. Plenty of space and some facilities to hand.

Armação de Pêra

Armação de Pêra: below the main promenade there is a good stretch of beach, although not too deep, with plenty of amenities. The fishermen use the east end of the beach where the access is easier and further east still there is plenty of untamed beach stretching all the way to Galé.

Cova Redonda

Cova Redonda: this small picturesque sandy cove is buried between high cliffs but there is a road which

Colourful cliffs at Praia da Marinha

leads down to it. A tunnel cut through the headland to the west gives access on foot to the adjacent beach of Senhora da Rocha described below.

Senhora da Rocha

Senhora da Rocha: again enclosed by steep cliffs but somewhat larger than the adjacent Cova Redonda. It is a very attractive setting enhanced by the little white church of Senhora da Rocha on the promontory. A problem here is that access is by a long flight of steps.

Praia da Marinha

Praia da Marinha: this is one of Algarve's most picturesque beaches often pictured in magazines or on front covers. This double cove enclosed by brightly hued cliffs is fairly isolated but easily reached by car. Steps lead down to this beautiful beach which has just enough facilities.

Carvoeira

Carvoeira: a small but attractive cove with plenty of facilities which is nowhere near large enough to accommodate the mass of visitors who stay in the immediate area.

Praia da Rocha

Praia da Rocha: attractive beach and promenade to this popular resort area. Steps at some parts but a ramp down in the central area. Loads of space on this beach of fine, soft sand and plenty of eating facilities at the rear all interconnected by wooden walkways.

Praia do Vau

Praia do Vau: this is another picturesque beach with a long stretch of sand enclosed by a line of undulating cliffs. There is easy access at the low point and plenty of amenities on hand.

Praia do Alvor

Praia do Alvor: a long, long stretch of fine sand backed by dunes and a broad scattering of cafés; easy access.

Meia Praia

Meia Praia: another endless stretch of fine sand backed by dunes, with limited facilities but being developed. This beach is used by holidaymakers arriving by ferry from Lagos. There is a large car park available for road users and access to the beach is then across the railway line.

Praia Dona Ana

Praia Dona Ana: a small but attractive beach, scattered with rock formations, which is well used in season; facilities to hand. Other sandy coves can be reached on foot either right or left of this one.

Praia da Luz

Praia da Luz: a fine, sandy beach with good access and amenities.

Salema

Salema: a large expanse of fine sand with easy access. Restaurants and facilities immediately to hand.

Some of the main towns and resorts in Algarve are well worth a visit. All those described here can be reached by public transport, either bus or train, although a car might be useful for some of the suggested side trips.

FARO

A s the capital city of Algarve, Faro is the administrative heart of the region and the hub of the bus and rail system.

Outer Faro is an uninteresting modern sprawl but in the middle lies an old town with its share of historic buildings, fine architecture and museums. Close by is a vibrant, pedestrianised shopping area with a wide ranging choice of merchandise. Here, cheerful parasols cluster amongst the surrounding bustle, a welcome oasis when it is time to indulge in that well-loved Portuguese pastime, coffee and cakes. In truth, half a day is enough to take in the sights and atmosphere of Faro as the area of interest is fairly compact.

Morning is the best time to visit, especially as afternoons become quite hot in summer, so go early before everything grinds to a halt for lunch. This leaves the rest of the day free for the beach, maybe the one out at Praia de Faro. Those with energy to spare might fancy a trip on the bus to Estói, for a stroll round the palace gardens and a visit to the Roman ruins of Milreu.

Faro flourished under the Moors and continued to do so later with the help of a large Jewish community. With the expulsion of the Jews from Portugal at the end of the fifteenth century, Faro might have lost its commercial cutting edge had it not been given city status and sixteen years later, in 1556, elevated to capital of Algarve. Its position was further

Faro gets its name

O ld Faro sits on a small mound nosing out into the Ria Formosa Reserve lagoon which is protected from the worst ravages of the sea by a rim of barrier islands. A fishing community occupied the site of Faro even before the Phoenicians. It became important under the Romans, who gave it the name Ossonoba. With the decline of the Roman Empire, the Visigoths took control and renamed the town Santa Maria. Their tenure lasted for three hundred years before the Moors swept in and, by the time they too were ejected by Dom Afonso III in 1249, Faro was known as Santa Maria de Hárune. It is thought the name Faro stems from a degradation of Hárune, the name of a Moorish governor, possibly through Faarom to Faro.

Continued on page 44...

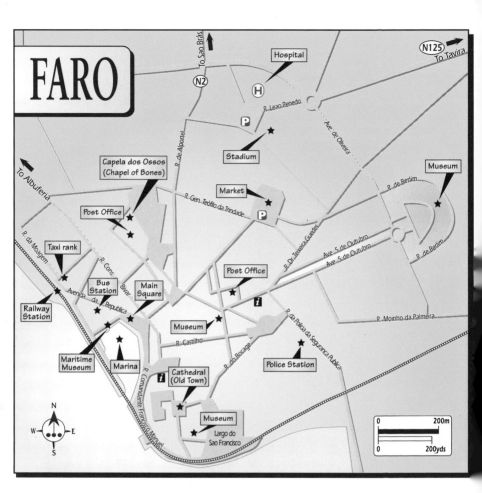

FARO

- Hospital
- To São Brás — N2
- N125 — To Tavira
- To Albufeira
- R. Leão Penedo
- Ave. de Oliveira
- Stadium
- Capela dos Ossos (Chapel of Bones)
- R. de Berlim
- Museum
- R. Gen. Teófilo da Trindade
- Market
- Post Office
- R. de Alportel
- R. da Modgem
- Taxi rank
- R. Cons.
- R. Dr. Teixeira Guedes
- Post Office
- Ave. 5 de Outubro
- Ave. 5 de Outubro
- R. de Berlim
- Bus Station
- Bivar
- Main Square
- Avenida da Republica
- Railway Station
- R. Moinho da Palmeira
- Museum
- R. Castilho
- Maritime Museum
- Marina
- R. do Bocage
- R. da Policia da Segurança Publica
- Police Station
- R. Comandante Francisco Manuel
- Cathedral (Old Town)
- N
- W — E
- S
- Museum
- Largo do Sao Francisco
- 0   200m
- 0   200yds

ILHA DESERTA

Opposite page:
Faro Marina

Above: Faro
pedestrianised
shopping area

Right: Faro
Promenade

Left: Faro   Right: Entrance to the Old Town, Faro (Arco da Vila)

strengthened in 1577 when the Bishopric of Algarve was transferred from Silves to Faro.

In 1596, whilst under Spanish domination, the city was sacked by the Earl of Essex but repaired itself and continued to prosper. The earthquakes of 1722 and 1755 all but destroyed it yet again. Rebuilding was set in motion and despite various setbacks, mainly regarding the country's internal political wrangling, Faro survived. Today's rapid expansion is largely due to wealth from tourism and Portugal's membership of the EU.

Tour of Faro

The Marina makes a natural starting place for any tour. By the side of the Marina in the harbourmaster's office,

past Hotel Eva, is the **Maritime Museum**. Besides models of ships, the museum is a great place to find out about the old methods of fishing, helped by exhibits with descriptions in English.

Inland from the marina, through the square, lies the pedestrianised shopping area but further east, beyond the **Jardim Manuel Bivar**, lies old Faro (Vila-a-Dentro). Entrance is through the eighteenth-century **Arco da Vila** with its niche for a statue of Saint Thomas Aquinas, the city's patron saint, which was a castle gate before the 1755 earthquake. Located next to the gateway is Turismo, opposite which is the Misericórdia church. Once through the gate, the narrow Rua do Município heads up past the Town Hall, on the left, into

Largo da Sé. Close by to the left is the location of Restaurante Cidade Velha, a delightful gourmet experience but heavy on the purse.

Orange trees add a splash of colour and a statue of Dom Francisco Gomes, the bishop who did much towards repairing the earthquake damage of 1755, gazes upon the Cathedral (Sé). The earliest settlement of Faro was probably upon this site where the Romans built a forum and the Visigoths later built their church of Santa Maria. A Moorish mosque followed but the present building was founded in the thirteenth century. The **Cathedral**, a patchwork of Romanesque, Gothic, Renaissance and Baroque, lost the top section of its tower in the earthquake. Internal decoration consists of gilded carving and blue *azulejos*

On the seaward side of the square is the **Bishop's Palace**. The street alongside passes down through the Arco da Porta Nova to reach the jetty where boats leave for Praia de Faro. Flower decked alleyways unfold a slower tempo of life where locals gather in the shade to pass the time of day.

Behind the Cathedral leads to Praça Dom Afonso III and the **Archaeological Museum** in the sixteenth-century Convent of Our Lady of the Assumption. The attractive two-level cloister is the setting for a display of Roman finds from Faro, Milreu and various sites in Algarve, *azulejos* and other interesting exhibits. From the museum, head down right to leave the old town through the Arco do Repouso.

Local fairs and festas are held in the **Largo de São Francisco** to the right, which is overlooked by the seventeenth-century church of the same name containing gilded wood carvings and the life of St Francis depicted in *azulejos*. For an insight into earlier life in the region make for Praça da Liberdade and the **Folklore Museum**. The exhibits include handicrafts, costumes, models of home interiors and old photographs, which are well presented. If church decoration appeals, the once humble fishermen's chapel of São Pedro, later elevated to a more decorative edifice, is worth a visit and is usually open for a couple of hours midday.

Fate in store

The main draw to this part of the city though has a more ghoulish intent. Although the impressive Baroque façade and glistening gilded interior of the Church of Carmo catch the eye, visitors are drawn to the **Capela dos Ossos** (Chapel of Bones) adjoining. Even the inscription above the doorway, which translates to – 'Stop here and think of the fate that will befall you', does little to deter those coming for sight of a room covered with the skulls and bones of monks removed from an adjacent cemetery in 1816. To reach the churches from the Folklore museum, head through Praça Ferreira de Almeida, an area noted for its typical Algarvian fish restaurants, towards the post office and Largo do Carmo.

• ALGARVE'S NATURE RESERVES •

Ria Formosa Natural Park.

Visitors arriving by air into Faro airport enjoy an absorbing birds-eye-view down over an extensive maze of salt marshes, waterways, mud flats, interlinked islands and lagoons which make up the Parque Natural Ria Formosa.

A large part of the park, located just east of Olhão, is open to visitors (9am-12noon and 2-5pm. Closed Saturday, Sunday and public holidays). A map showing the routes around the reserve and indicating points of interest can be obtained at the information building where there is also an exhibition featuring the activities within the reserve and a café.

The reserve is rich in wild flowers and birds with hides for the bird watchers. There is a restored tidal mill, garum tanks left by the Romans and the park is involved in conservation breeding to preserve the *Cão de Água*, the Portuguese water dog.

Castro Marim Nature Reserve

Near Vila Real, this reserve occupies the old *salinas*, the salt pans used for extracting sea salt by evaporation. It is a great place for bird spotters and one of the commonest birds is the black-winged stilt, the symbol of the reserve. Flamingos are around too and storks, but this is a place to settle down with binoculars to see the most species. A new Reserve building is located on the banks of the Guadiana River near Castro Marim.

Quinta do Lago Nature Trails

Lying on the western edge of the Ria Formosa reserve, they are not well signposted but can be found by heading first for Quinta do Lago and following signs for Praia and Quinta do Lago Hotel. This leads through the Planal estate and over endless roundabouts before terminating at a car park and the starting point of both trails.

Set amongst woodland, salt marsh and dunes, these two nature trails are laid out with information points to increase awareness of the diversity of flora and fauna. The blue Quinta do Lago trail, a walk in total of 1.6 miles (2.5km), heads out in a westerly direction and the yellow São Lourenço trail, a little shorter at 1.25 miles (2km), heads east.

ALBUFEIRA

Albufeira is an international resort attracting many visitors. For those resident elsewhere in the province, it is a worthwhile excursion which, with a little time set aside for relaxing on the beach, can easily fill a day.

Albufeira

White houses and villas may fill the surrounding hillsides but all the activity in this cosmopolitan resort is focused down in the older central area by the sea front. Pedestrianised walkways, attractively paved in small, hand cut marble blocks (*calçada*), and cheerfully lined with souvenir shops, bars, restaurants and pavement cafés encourage browsing. Although there are pubs and fast food outlets in plenty, the insistence a few years ago on removing English signs has done much to improve its image. Apart from enjoying the ambience, there are one or two things to see including the beach, the fishermen's beach and the old town with the remains of the castle.

Baltum it was called when the Romans first settled here and built a castle. Later, when the Moors took over from the Visigoths, they renamed it Al-Buheira meaning the Castle on the Sea. It prospered as a trading port under the Moors for almost five centuries until it returned to the hands of the Christians first in 1189 but finally in 1250. The instant loss of its North African trade brought poverty in its wake but, over the centuries, it started to prosper again as a fishing village.

Throughout the Middle Ages the castle remained important in the safeguarding and protection of the town, especially when the coastline was harassed by French and English privateers. The massive earthquake of 1755 that flattened Lisbon also severely damaged Albufeira and its castle. Just as severe was the damage inflicted on the town in 1833 by the Miguelist guerrillas after a siege and battle that was part of the War of the Two Brothers.

Fish, particularly tuna and sardines, and the birth of the canning industry brought a new wave of prosperity in the late nineteenth century which carried through until around 1930. At this time a decline set in which was reversed by the growth of a totally new industry, tourism, and the rest, as they say, is history.

Tour of Albufeira

Right in the heart of town is the large square of Largo Eng. Duarte Pacheco, which is decked out with fountains and decorative beds of exotic birds-of-paradise flowers. This is a good place to start a tour. Head out into the pedestrianised shop-lined Rua 5 de Outubro that leads towards the sea front and the main beach. On the left near the bottom is the location of the tourist office and beyond there the road enters a short tunnel through the rock beneath the Sol e Mar Hotel to the promenade overlooking the beach. Admire this splendid beach by all means but put temptation aside for the moment and continue the tour by returning through the tunnel and climbing the stairs by the tourist office to reach the upper level. Head left here to enter the region of the old town, which was once enclosed within the castle.

Azulejos tile panels on the wall mark the position of the various entrances to the old castle, like Porta da Praça almost opposite the entrance to the Sol e Mar Hotel. Wandering back and forth down the narrow cobbled streets takes no time at all in the confined area of the old town and it has its rewards. The sixteenth-century Chapel of the Misericórdia, thought to be built on the site of a mosque, lies down Rua

Above: Good choice of street cafés, Albufeira
Below: Lively square in Albufeira

Henrique Calado and is worth passing to see the beautiful Manueline doorway. Wandering down Travessa de Igreja Velha leads beneath an arch, which was once part of the castle and shortly Ruinas restaurant is reached. This restaurant is built in what was a tower of the castle although this is perhaps best appreciated by viewing from across the adjacent Fishermen's Beach.

Fishermen's Beach is one of the more colourful corners of Albufeira where jumpered fishermen work, silently untangling nets while scantily clad bathers are bent on nothing

more than pleasure and relaxation; a meeting of two worlds. Rua Cândido dos Reis leads around the back of the old town to the main square where the tour started.

If time allows, there is a chance to catch up on some shopping at the excellent daily fruit and vegetable market just north of the dual carriageway road which rings the rear of the town. It is signposted from the road and well used by the locals but is best in the mornings. Also along this ring road are two large supermarkets.

Left: The main beach at Albufeira

Below: Albufeira; fishermans beach

TAVIRA

Located east of Faro, Tavira is a riverside working town which unconsciously blends charm and history. The fun way to arrive is by train from Faro, a journey that takes around fifty minutes, but allows time to take in some of the scenery of eastern Algarve.

Cacela Velha

Stroll beneath the palms alongside the river, explore the medieval bridge, the old castle, some fine architecture in the town's churches or take a trip on the ferry to the Ilha de Tavira for a spot of swimming or sunbathing. A half day is more than enough for sightseeing and visitors with a car can make interesting side trips either west to Santa Luzia and Pedras d'el Rei from where the miniature train chuffs out to Barril on Ilha de Tavira or east to Cabanas or Cacela Velha.

Tavira's early history is uncertain but the Romans were here and built a bridge over the river to carry a road connecting their settlements at Ossanoba (Faro) and Myrtilis (Mértola). Only the foundations now remain since the present structure is medieval. Under the Moors the town flourished as a port and continued to do so after the Christians regained the territory in 1242.

Prosperity and disaster

Almonds, carobs, figs and the scarlet dye extracted from the kermes oak became major exports for a time but a series of disasters struck the town leading to a serious decline in prosperity. The river started to silt up, plague struck in 1645 and the great earthquake of 1755 seriously damaged the buildings. Tuna fishing and the canning industry brought something of a revival at the end of the nineteenth century but overfishing and protests over the brutal method of netting and harpooning the tuna brought this to a close in 1972.

Tour of Tavira

The old arched bridge spanning the river still seems to be a focal point of the town even though there is a new bridge further south taking the main traffic flow. Flooding caused considerable damage to the ancient structure in the winter of 1989/90 but it has since been restored and is now used only by pedestrians and cyclists. Strolling across the bridge to the east bank gives perhaps the best view of the old walled town and castle which sits on top of a small rise.

Praça da República, on the west bank, is where much of the activity seems to take place. Walking down through the palm shaded, riverside gardens leads to the old market hall now converted into shops and cafés.

The new market is further down still, to the right of the new bridge.

There are scant remains of the castle to see but a wander around the old part offers a chance to see some of the interesting buildings in the town. Head inland from the west side of the old bridge to find Rua da Galeria which is the location of the tourist office. This attractive alley passes beneath the archway known as Arco da Misericórdia decorated with a granite crest and armillary spheres, the symbol of Dom Manuel. Directly through the arch is the Misericórdia church which will probably be locked but the sixteenth-century portal with the saints Peter and Paul is there to be admired. Beyond are the remains of the castle from where there are good views of Tavira over the 'Pombaline' terracotta rooftops of the houses. This distinctive, almost oriental style of four pitched roof was used extensively in the rebuilding instigated by Pombal after the earthquake of 1755, which did so much damage to the country. Also here is the **church of Santa Maria do Castelo** which was built originally on the site of a mosque in the thirteenth century. Some of the Gothic elements remain in the doorway and inside is the tomb of Paio Peres Correia who led the assault which liberated Tavira from the Moors.

Excursions west of Tavira

Santa Luzia is just a short journey by car reached by following along the coast. Still very much a fishing village, it has an attractive, palm-lined promenade that lends a touch of the exotic. It lies on an inland channel usually littered with fishing boats and is protected from the open sea by the Ilha de Tavira sandbar. Amongst the fishing gear left around, it is not unusual to see piles of crustacean covered terracotta pots with a thick-rimmed wide mouth (*alcatruzes*) that are used for catching octopus. It is a great place to relax with a drink at one of the cafés on the sea front and idly watch the activities of the fishermen.

Just a little further west is **Pedras d'el Rei**, the starting point for the miniature train which chugs over to Barril on Ilha de Tavira. A pontoon bridge leads from the car park across a watery channel to the small station at the terminal of this single line, narrow gauge railway. A central passing place allows trains to plough back and forward when the demand is there. Walking the paved path over

Above: Fishing boat at Tavira
Below: Santa Luzia

to Barril takes only around 15/20 minutes and entertainment along the way is provided by the antics of the fiddler crabs on the mud banks.

Barril is just a small settlement amidst acres of fine golden sand with restaurant/café facilities and sun-beds and shades for those in need.

Excursions east of Tavira

There are two places to explore just east of Tavira which can easily be reached by car, these are Cabanas and Cacela Velha.

Tourist accommodation crowds the rear of **Cabanas** but ignore this and head for the sea front. An old atmosphere still prevails around the huddle of village houses and fishing is still an important occupation. It is protected from the open sea by a sand spit that extends eastwards eventually to join the mainland near Manta Rosa. It is possible to walk out to this sand bar at low tide from the eastern edge of the village near the forgotten fort that guards the estuary. Unfortunately, the fort is not open to the public but from its appearance it would appear to date from the seventeenth/eighteenth century.

Tiny **Cacela Velha**, near Manta Rosa, is all atmosphere with a dazzling white church and a miniature eighteenth-century fortress. It clings together on a perch looking over a lagoon which can be reached by steps down an easy tree lined slope.

Above: Santa Luzia
Below: Tavira riverside

LAGOS

Busy riverside Lagos conjures up an air of elegance and refinement which sets it apart from other resorts in Algarve. It can easily be reached by bus and train and is well worth a day's exploration. Apart from enjoying the ambience, it has an excellent museum with many artefacts from the Roman period, old town walls to see, a small fort to inspect and a lighthouse surrounded by some of the most dramatic coastline in Algarve, full of stacks and intriguing rock formations. The latter destination is a short walk out of town.

Lagos

As a safe port in an estuary location, Lagos has seen the footprints of many traders through the centuries, from the Phoenicians, Greeks and Carthaginians to the Romans who called the place Lacobriga.

When the Moors eventually took control in the eighth century, they renamed it Zawaya and defended the town with walls. From here the Moors built up a strong trade with North Africa to bring prosperity to the residents.

Unable to resist the Christian reconquest, Lagos was recovered by Dom Afonso II in 1249 but its history does not stop there. Dom Dinis recognised its potential value as a port so, in the fourteenth century, he ordered the castle to be rebuilt and the walls raised. In 1415, a mighty fleet of Portuguese ships assembled here for a successful assault on Ceuta in Morocco. This brought Henry the Navigator onto the scene who came to Lagos to gather about him a team of pilots, cartographers and navigators before setting up a school at Sagres (see the feature box on page 58).

Early succession

Young Dom Sebastião was quite captivated by Lagos and decided to make it the capital of Algarve. There is now a rather curious statue of him in the main square. He came to the throne at the age of three and grew up rather headstrong and full of crusading zeal. In 1578, at the age of 24, he led an ill equipped and unprepared Portuguese army against powerful Muslim forces in North Africa. At the Battle of Alcácer on 4 August, he was killed along with another 8,000 Portuguese soldiers, including many young nobles, and twice as many were taken prisoner. It was a devastating blow for the country, which ultimately brought the demise of the House of Avis since his successor, the 66-year-old Cardinal Henrique, lived only a further two years and died childless.

Like other places in Algarve, Lagos suffered badly in the great earthquake of 1755. Although rebuilt, it was never quite able to regain its former glory and settled for a quiet life of fishing. Towards the end of the nineteenth century there was an upsurge of activity with the introduction of canning factories and the town returned to prosperity. At its peak, Lagos had some forty canning factories but overfishing brought an inevitable decline. Tourism is bringing a new wave of prosperity and it looks set for continued success.

Tour of Lagos

Start a walking tour in the main square named after Gil Eanes, one of the town's famous explorers, which is marked by the stone statue of a pink-faced Dom Sebastião. Love it or hate it, it succeeds more than most statues in that it gets noticed. Somehow, the young king in his suit of armour manages to look more like a modern biker. The middle road on the south side leads into the main pedestrianised Rua 25 de Abril filled with pavement cafés. Souvenir, craft and antique shops fill the broad main street brightened by bright parasols and tables.

Resist spending too much time here for the moment and continue ahead and slightly right into Rua da Silva Lopes which ends outside the **church of Santo António**, also the museum. Completed originally in the eighteenth century, the church was restored after the earthquake of 1755 and retains its fine Baroque carvings. Fat-faced cherubs hide amongst the elaborate gilded woodwork on the upper walls but the lower walls are decorated with *azulejos* panels depicting scenes from the life of Santo

Above: *shopping in Lagos*
Below: *The Aquabus at Lagos Marina*

• Infante Dom Henrique – Henry the Navigator •

1394-1460

Henry was the third son of Dom João 1 and Philippa of Lancaster, daughter of John of Gaunt, Duke of Lancaster. His parents' marriage cemented the Treaty of Windsor in 1386. This was signed as a declaration of lasting peace between the two countries after English help at the Battle of Aljubarrota in 1385, which secured Portugal's independence from Spain.

As a child, Henry grew up close to the Douro riverside in Porto (Oporto) where his curiosity in seafaring matters was most likely aroused. It was here he probably first encountered tales of the legendary Christian Kingdom of Prester John, and its untold riches, said to lie somewhere in Africa.

In 1415, Henry supervised a Crusade to Ceuta in North Africa and set sail from Porto with his father and brother. They returned victorious and a lasting impression on Henry was not so much the victory itself but the oriental riches they looted. Although Henry focused his interest on taming the north coast of Africa, he became a landlubber. Only later, on hearing tales from other sailors, did his ambitions to search further afield develop.

Taking himself off down to the untamed wilds of Sagres in Algarve, Henry established an observatory and school of navigation, where he devoted time, effort and money to improving navigational aids and boat design. He gathered together experts in astronomy and astrology, cartography and geography as well as knowledgeable mariners. His shipyard at Lagos built the boats, from where they set sail.

To pursue his quest, in 1443 Henry was given a grant of land at Cabo de São Vicente, which included Sagres, by his brother Dom Pedro, who was regent at the time. Trading gradually took over precedence from crusading as Henry developed a tidy business from financing and equipping excursions down the west coast of Africa. This was helped by a new boat, the *Caravel*, which Henry and his team designed and perfected. This new boat was faster and easier to control and could also move close inshore.

Under Henry's patronage Gil Eanes, of Lagos, finally passed Cape Bojador on Africa's west coast in 1434, a barrier beyond which fifteen earlier expeditions had been too afraid to penetrate. Trade expanded and explorers returned with samples of plant life, fruit and nuts. It was to be a further decade before Gil Eanes returned with the first human cargo of African slaves, which prompted an escalation of trade along the west coast of Africa.

By the time he died at Sagres in 1460, his expeditions had reached as far as Sierra Leone.

António. Those with their eyes down might notice the name of the Irishman Hugo Beaty on one of the tombstones making up the floor. He was the commander of a regiment once quartered in the town.

A side door in the church leads into the museum. It is a little unfortunate that the excellent exhibits are accompanied only by information in Portuguese. Although only small, it is one of the most interesting museums in the region. It tells the story of life and culture of old Algarve through models with the aid of relics and artefacts and has a more historical section with mosaics, frescos, pottery and Corinthian capitals from the Roman period, some from nearby Vila Abicada, and Bronze Age relics from Vila do Bispo.

Early European slave trade

Turn towards the riverside on leaving the museum to enter Praça da República for a view of the slave market, **Mercado dos Esravos**, which is now a small gallery at the confluence of two roads on the north side. When the caravels set sail from Lagos in search of treasures they also brought back a human cargo in the form of slaves. This market has the dubious distinction of being the very first place in Europe to sell slaves.

Walking south now along the riverside gives a good view of the castellated town walls that dominate the statue of Gil Eanes, the famous explorer. Further down, at the estuary of the Ribeira de Bensafrim, lies the **Fort of Ponta da Bandeira**. Built in the seventeenth century, this compact fort barely looks large enough to defend the entrance to the river but it has now been restored and welcomes invaders in the form of tourists, for a small charge. There is a poster museum inside dedicated to Henry the Navigator, which is fairly uninspiring and one to miss if time is short. On the seaward side of the fort is a tiny beach but for a better beach, take the summertime ferry across the river to Meia Praia.

Ponta da Piedade lies out of town to the south and can be reached on foot but it takes around forty minutes. One way is to keep following the coast road, then pick up the signs, but the slightly quicker way is through town. From the slave market pass the church of Santo António and keep ahead up through the narrow streets turning left to leave the town through a gateway in the walls. Follow signs now along the road passing very close to Dona Ana beach, which makes a good resting place for one or both legs of the journey.

Stations of the cross line the road leading towards the lighthouse. Here the coastline is truly spectacular with its weird rock shapes and stacks used as breeding grounds by the birds, especially egrets that are common in the province. There is a narrow footbridge to lead the intrepid out a little further for even more dramatic views but this is not recommended for people who suffer from vertigo.

SILVES

Sitting on a hill alongside the River Arade, atmospheric Silves is an old Moorish town still boasting a very fine castle and cathedral. Half a day is enough time to enjoy the ambience of the town and take in the sights. Buses connect Silves to Albufeira and Portimão and there is also the train, although the station is a rather inconvenient 2 miles (3km) south of the town. More romantically, it is possible to catch an excursion boat up the river from Portimão when the tide is suitable.

Silves

Silves has been a settlement for a very long time, especially since its river was more navigable in the past than it is at present. Finds from the Neolithic and Bronze Ages suggest settlement as early as 900BC when the Phoenicians were around. Metal ores may have been one of the attractions and there is one mine shaft started on top of the hill. This is now inside the castle and known as the Dog's Cistern, and can be traced back to this period. Coins found in Silves bearing the word Cylpes were minted in Silves around 206-240 BC by a Celtic-Cylpense tribe.

Place of importance

By the time the Romans arrived, it is likely that the hill top position was already fortified and they adopted and strengthened it to make Silves into an important centre. It developed even further under the Arabs into an important maritime trading port sending out great cargoes of citrus fruit, figs, fish, timber and cork. Such was its importance that it became the capital of Algarve for a time. Fine buildings grew apace, the castle was strengthened to match the town's importance and it attracted men of wealth and culture, including writers and poets.

All was not necessarily peace and harmony. Towards the end of the Moorish period, the people of Silves were often drawn into petty squabbles between rival Arab factions. A great battle took place on 3 September 1189 when Dom Sancho I strove to regain the town for the Christians. He was assisted by crusaders including King Richard the Lion Heart from England and King Philip II of France. Victory was achieved, although not easily, but the Moors returned to retake the town just two years later. It was not until 1249 that Silves along with Faro and Algarve as a whole were eventually recovered by the Portuguese.

Although Silves was rebuilt and its castle restored, it never achieved its former prosperity. Shipping trade slipped away to Portimão when the river slowly started to silt up, restricting passage to smaller vessels. A whole series of earthquakes, six in the fourteenth century, more in the sixteenth century and two especially severe ones in 1722 and 1755, decimated the town, reducing it to a mere village of 200 inhabitants. It has grown again, its castle has been restored and it occupies an important role at the hub of the orange trade from which it earns most of its wealth.

Tour of Silves

The riverside is a good place to start, by the arched medieval bridge believed to have been built over a similar Roman structure. It needs a flight of imagination to see the tall ships loading up their cargo at this sleepy quayside, which now serves only pleasure boats from Portimão. Near the quay is the bustling market hall teeming with local produce and is the place to buy oranges when in season. Early shopping is essential to get the best choice but, in any case, most daily markets like this one tend to close at lunch.

Above: **Silves Castle**
Below: **English factory (Cultural Centre)**
Opposite page: **Praça do Municipio, Silves**

The cafés and eating places crowding the front of the market are where locals gather for serious conversation and eating. Outside grills are busy barbecuing chicken or thick slices of fatty bacon generating heady aromas of delicious food and mixed with clouds of burning smoke.

Cobbled streets lead uphill from the market area towards the middle of town that lies over to the right. Entering the main square along Rua 25 Abril one passes the tourist office, which usually has a leaflet available containing a town plan and highlighting points of interest. Looking rather like an Italian piazza, the main square, Praça do Municipio, is where the locals and tourists gather lazily at shaded tables to drink coffee, chat and generally watch the world go by.

An inviting gateway through the robust stone tower, Torreão das Portas da Cicade, which was once part of the old city walls leads into Rua da Sé and another uphill climb. This narrow cobbled street bounded by white balconied houses leads up to the cathedral. Lying opposite the cathedral is the misericórdia church which has a beautiful Manueline doorway puzzlingly raised well above ground level. At this height, the doorway was able to accept a coffin directly from the back of a cart and it is still common practice for the deceased to lie in church on the night preceding burial.

Further up the hill is the red sandstone castle and waiting inside to greet visitors is a powerful statue of Dom Sancho I clasping an unsheathed sword. If he appeared like that when he first liberated Silves from the Moors in 1189, he would have struck fear into the heart of his opponents. Steps to the left of the statue lead up to the southern rampart from where it is possible to walk the full perimeter of the castle walls, through the various towers and turrets, while enjoying some spectacular views over the surrounding countryside.

Silves Cathedral

Originally in Gothic style, earthquakes over the centuries have taken their toll of the cathedral and the various restorations, particularly the one after the massive earthquake of 1755, have destroyed the architectural unity. Compare the elegance of the Gothic chancel with gauche Baroque rebuilding of the nave completed after 1755. There is a stone marking the grave of Dom João II who died in Alvor in 1495 and was buried here, although his remains were later transferred to Batalha Abbey. The side chapel to the right of the main entrance contains the tombs of two friends of Henry the Navigator whilst the rest of the tombs belong to bishops.

Within the interior of the castle lies the Cistern of the Enchanted Moorish Girl, which is of uncertain origin. Only part of the arched ceiling can be seen above ground but below there is a huge chamber, 55ft (18m) long and 47ft (14.5m) wide, with a ceiling made up of three vaults supported on pillars. Nearby there are some ongoing excavations, which as yet reveal nothing of particular interest. A focal point within the castle grounds is the Dog's Cistern, over to the west side, which is the shaft of a former mine exploited by both the Romans and the Moors although there is a popular belief that it contains a secret tunnel to the riverside.

Leaving the castle by the one and only gate, turn left down steps to find Café Inglês beneath the castle walls. Enjoy refreshments on the terrace by all means, but if the roof garden is open, it is worth trying the brandy and almond chocolate St Emillion dessert up there just to enjoy the prospect of the castle walls and the cathedral from that viewpoint.

Heading back to the main square, turn left just before the gateway through Torreão das Portas da Cicade to find the modern museum. It has been especially constructed around an old Moorish well on Rua das Portas and contains a selection of archaeological artefacts but the interest is again diminished for many visitors by the fact that the information is presented only in Portuguese.

Save time for the **Fábrica do Inglês** the old cork factory now converted into a cultural centre. The complex is developed around a quadrangle with one side of the factory retained to house a museum devoted to cork. A varied selection of snack bars, cafés and restaurants line the rest of the square with a Tea House surrounded by orange trees the central feature. A programme of cultural events and street entertainment runs throughout the summer months and occasionally in winter.

Among other attractions are tours of Silves by miniature train, wine tasting and a childrens' playground. Entrance to the complex is free unless there is a special event taking place. All facilities open all day every day in summer. In winter, cafés and restaurants close for a couple of days each week but rotate their days off so there is always something open.

• FUN DAYS OUT FOR THE FAMILY •

Water Theme Parks

These are quite a feature in Algarve and there are a number of them strung across the province. Spiralling water chutes and giant multi-lane water slides are central to the facilities provided, which also include swimming pools with wave machines and possibly other amusements to make the park attractive to the whole family. Restaurants and bars cater for every need and there are sun loungers and shades provided to encourage visitors to stay throughout the day. Apart from the major theme parks listed below, there are other smaller ones near major areas of tourism:

Aqualine: in the east of Algarve on the N125, on the inland side of the road just beyond Altura travelling east. This one has a full complement of chutes and slides providing plenty of fun for the family.

Atlantico: on the N125 at Almancil, just west of Faro. Another park with chutes, slides and waves.

The Big One: on the N125 at Alcantarilha, just west of Albufeira. This one is spacious with 15 acres (60,000 sq m) of shaded and landscaped gardens and has all the necessary slides and chutes including a cork-screw.

Slide and Splash: this was on the main N125 just west of Lagoa until a new by-pass road was built which now makes it necessary to turn onto the Estombar road. It is one of the largest with a special bus to collect visitors from Albufeira, Carvoeira, Portimão area, Lagos, Armação de Pêra, Quarteira and Sagres. For bus times, which usually include a morning run and an early afternoon pickup, and possible reservations, ☎ 282 322 827. Their park offers a wide range of chutes and slides with enticing names like the corkscrew, torpedo, whizzer and when those are done, it is good to finish on cloud 9.

Zoo park

Zoomarine: on the N125 at Guia, just west of Albufeira. This is a real mixed bag of entertainment with regular shows by performing sea lions and dolphins and even parrots, a small fun fair for children, a swimming pool, mini golf and many other attractions to keep children amused all day long.

Left: English factory (Cultural Centre)

Below left: Silves main square

Below right: Dom Sancho I statue in the castle

Places to Visit

In the Towns

Faro

Maritime Museum
Open 9.15am-12noon and 2-4.30pm.
Closed Saturday, Sunday and public
holidays.

Cathedral
Open 10am-12noon and 2-5pm. Closed
Saturday, Sunday and public holidays.

Archaeological Museum
In the 16th century Convent of Our
Lady of the Assumption.
Open 9am-12noon and 2-5pm. Closed
Saturday, Sunday and public holidays.

Folklore Museum
9.30am-12.30pm and 2.30-5.30pm.
Closed Saturday, Sunday and public
holidays.

Lagos

Museum
At the church of Santo António
Open 9.30am-12.30pm and 2-5pm.
Closed Monday and public holidays.
A small charge is made.

Fort of Ponta da Bandeira
Open 10am-1pm and 2-6pm, Sunday
10am-1pm. Closed Monday and public
holidays.

Silves

Castle
Open daily 9am-7pm. Closed public
holidays.

Museum
Open 10am-12.30pm and 2.30-6pm
daily. Closed public holidays.

Fábrica do Inglês
Cultural centre just a few minutes
walk along the main road leading east
of the town. Has underground car
parking.
Open 10am-11pm daily
Cork museum at the centre.
Open 9.30am-1pm and 2-6.30pm
daily.

The five tours described here start in the west and sweep eastwards to cover the main highlights as well as including some of the nooks and crannies. Those able to follow them all will gain a good overall feel for the region. Popular tours are those which include the highest mountain Fóia, at Monchique, and the westerly cape of Sagres but the lesser known historic town of Mértola, just over the border in Alentejo, is outstanding.

CAR TOUR 1:
WAY OUT WEST TO SAGRES.

Towering cliffs, wind-cut vegetation, two old forts and a lighthouse dominate the landscape in the extreme west which thrusts defiantly into the Atlantic. A sense of an older Algarve can still be found in lesser developed old fishing villages like Burgau and Salema. Strands of fine sand and secluded coves are also a feature amongst the convolutions of this rugged coastline. The promontory at the tip has been cloaked in myth and mystery since ancient times and was *Promontorium Sacrum* (Sacred Cape) to the Romans who also believed it to be the end of the earth.

Once regarded as a wild and inhospitable outpost, access to the west has been eased with the building of a by-pass around Portimão and extensive road improvements. Aptly referred to as the Barlavento (windward), although it does have its share of calm days, a full day is required to appreciate fully this remote corner of Algarve.

Follow the N125 from Lagos to Sagres but be prepared to turn off left to **Luz** before too long. The road wends seawards through the countryside towards a blindingly white development of villas and apartments which now huddles around the original fishing village. Follow signs to Praia to find the sea front car park but summer visitors may have to park on the outskirts and walk. Luz is still small scale, with a good beach and ready access to coastal walking, and makes a pleasant place to stay for those in search of a more restful ambience. One of its more original restaurants is sited in the old fort 'Fortaleza' whilst excellent food is served at the comfortable Hotel Belavista da Luz, up the hill from the church back towards the N125.

Next stop is **Burgau** so again watch for the left turn. Some development has appeared on the approaches but the old village itself is hidden from view being tucked into a cleft in the cliff. Park along to the right at the top and walk. The narrow road leads steeply down between the old fishermen's cottages to the shore and a cluster of brightly painted fishing boats. A great place to sit for a coffee; in one of the small restaurant/café/bars which now pepper the village along with a few tourist shops. Fishing activity takes place mainly in the early morning for those looking for something more lively than a sleepy village.

Continuing west along the minor road parallel with the coast, which later becomes a track, leads to the beach at **Boca do Rio**. Remains of a Roman settlement lie here awaiting excavation. Once an area of salt pans and marsh, this area is a location for bird watchers, and overlooked by a derelict castle on a nearby hill.

Back on the N125, the left turn to **Salema** is soon reached once past Budens. Development is more in evidence here but not so intrusive once down by the shore in the heart of the old village. Unlike Burgau, the beach is more accessible and it is possible to drive close to the shore. A slower pace of life prevails and fishermen tend their boats and nets under the watchful eye of the old village ribboned up the hillside to the east. Visitors come to enjoy the vast expanse of sandy beach, stroll up the narrow village street out onto the headland or simply sit and soak in the atmosphere from the veranda of the restaurant edging the shore.

When the N125 again beckons, carry on west to pass through Figueira but keep an eye open in around 1.25 miles (2km) for the thirteenth-century **chapel of Nossa Senhora de Guadalupe** on the right, one of the oldest churches in Algarve. Henry the Navigator is thought to have worshipped here when he lodged in Raposeira for a while. A narrow road off left at Raposeira leads to the secluded beaches of Ingrina and Zavial. At Vila do Bispo, join the N268. This is the dividing of the ways on the return if you choose to return via Aljezur and Monchique. The road now leads speedily south to Sagres through a

Luz Church

Above left: Burgau

Above right: West coast at Castelejo near Sagres

Below: Fishermen, Sagres

cowering landscape ablaze with the hues of flowers in spring.

As civilisation starts to intrude, the looming white bastion on the skyline captures attention. This is **Sagres** and its fort. To the left at the roundabout lies the village and access down to **Baleeira** fishing harbour. Unbelievably, there is no shortage of good beaches in this wild spot but they are best saved for calm days. Most, like Mareta, Tonel and Beliche require negotiating cliff paths but Martinhal can easily be reached in a car by turning off left before reaching Sagres round-about.

Sagres was put on the map with the building of a fortress by Henry the Navigator, which is thought to have been the site of his School of Navigation (see feature box). Little remains from that time except the small church of Santa Maria and possibly the large wind compass, *Rosa dos Ventos*, which was uncovered in 1928. Henry's fortress and library were destroyed in 1587, along with the other forts in the area, by Sir Francis Drake when Portugal was under Spanish rule. Although recon-struction was put in hand in the following century thet were de-stroyed yet again, this time by the earthquake of 1755.

The present façade stems from half-hearted rebuilding at a time when it had outlived its usefulness. There is little to excite now beyond the entrance, except the death defy-ing antics of locals fishing above the boiling waters below the steep cliffs of the promontory. The church and wind compass remain but other old buildings have all but been destroyed and rebuilt. These now contain an exhibition hall of questionable value,

a café and a surprising selection of tasteful souvenirs and books in the shop upstairs.

The final push to the very tip of land at **Cape St Vincent** is soon achieved. Just before reaching the lighthouse is the smaller fort and restaurant of **Beliche** with access to a beach below. Vendors of woolly jumpers await at the cape. Visitors are allowed into the lighthouse grounds and there is chance to in-spect the lamps more closely if the keeper is around.

From Sagres there is only one way to go, back the same way, at least as far as Vila do Bispo. North to Aljezur passes through **Carrapateira** with access to superb sandy beaches, their only drawback being the wild-ness of the sea along this western coastline. A further option is to turn right on joining the N120, before reaching Aljezur, back to Lagos which passes through the typical Algarvian village of Bensafrim. Old Aljezur boasts a small ruined castle on a hill and the N267 heads east from here inland towards Monchique.

CAR TOUR 2:
THE HIGH PEAK TRAIL

For a green Algarve, head for the mountains of Serra de Monchique, to the very top of the highest, Fóia, but there is little to detain the visitor for long. For an interesting contrast and to make this excursion into a full day, coastal Portimão and surrounding resorts are also included in the tour. If the view from the mountain is important, try and choose a day when Fóia can be seen from Portimão

Azulejos on park bench, Portimao

Ultimately, there is one road leading northwards into Monchique, the N266, which can be joined at Portimão or, if travelling from the east of Algarve, via Silves. Once travelling on this road and climbing into the hills, the countryside takes on a greener hue even in summer. Plantations of the Australian eucalyptus trees with their blue-green leaves and peeling bark have changed the landscape along sections of this road as they have in many parts of Algarve. As the road twists its way up the mountains, watch out for the road left leading to Termas de Monchique (Caldas de Monchique) which is the first port of call.

Termas de Monchique (Caldas de Monchique) is an ancient atmospheric spa town lying in a wooded valley beneath a crook in the main road, from which it is barely visible. More recently it has been totally revamped, while still retaining the original façades, and its spa function revitalised. The short onward journey to Monchique passes some of the granite quarries which are important to the economy of the area.

Monchique remains something of an enigma. Fóia is the real draw but most visitors stop here to explore this mountain village yet it has singularly failed to capitalise on its assets. Recent years have seen some smartening of its appearance but the main square remains a dull affair despite the recent addition of a water feature. It is worth a stop to wander up the narrow cobbled Rua do Porto Fundo, leaving from the corner of the square near to the bus station, in search of wicker baskets or pottery. Entering this street then turning left up the first narrow alley and following signs leads eventually, after about fifteen minutes' walking, to the ru-

Portimao suspension bridge

ined convent of Nossa Senhora do Desterro. There is nothing to see at the convent but the reward for all the effort is some fine views back down over the town.

A good road leaves from the main square and winds up the mountainside to the dizzy heights of **Fóia**. Restaurants, chicken piri-piri being a popular choice on the menu, are passed on the way up. These offer the opportunity to take lunch while pouring over truly extensive views. Just before the summit is a *miradouro* which is best visited on the way down to avoid crossing the traffic.

A forest of aerials and communication masts covers the summit that reaches an altitude of 2960ft (902m). In their midst is a purpose built handicraft shop which seems to specialise in selling thick, warm jumpers but there are other craft items to see. The real purpose of visiting the summit is for the views, which on a clear day are extensive, taking in Portimão directly south and the whole of the coastline out towards Sagres and Cape St Vincent.

If freshly grilled sardines have not yet been sampled, then head back to Portimão for lunch by the riverside. There is an interesting off the beaten track route for the return, which has the advantage of using mostly narrow but good roads. Head south from Monchique but turn right shortly towards Marmelete and, 3.5 miles (5.6km) later on reaching Casais, turn left following a sign to Penina 12 miles (19km), and the N125.

Portimão is a bustling riverside port and industrial focus but it still attracts visitors for its waterfront atmosphere and good shopping. The bustling riverside atmosphere has diminished a little, now that the unloading of fish has transferred to the new port on the other side of the estuary. However there are still boats around tempting visitors to take trips up the river to Silves or offering the thrill and excitement of deep sea fishing.

Sardines

Catch the scent of grilling sardines on the wind and follow to source on the riverside near the old bridge at Portimão. Sardines grilling on pavement barbecues seem to be everywhere amongst this close huddle of restaurants, so wander around, inspect the fish and take your choice! Do not be surprised if they are served with boiled potatoes, it is traditional with sardines.

Shoppers will have no trouble finding the pedestrianised area around Rua Vasco da Gama where they can shop until they drop, finding bargains amongst the designer label clothes, shoes, exquisite crystal, leather goods or just spending the time window gazing.

Time to move on to nearby **Praia da Rocha** which can be reached simply by following along the coast. Interest in this popular resort area is entirely focused around the flower-decked promenade and sandy beach. At the eastern end, overlooking the estuary, is the small Forte of Santa Caterina, which is now partly occupied by a terrace café and restaurant.

Above: Portimao, grilling sardines

Right: Street side cáfe, Portimao

Praia da Rocha

There are fine views from here across the estuary to the other fortification guarding the entrance to the river, Castelo São João de Arade, which is where this tour finally concludes. Restaurants line the rear of the beach down at sand level which are all connected by walkways. At the western end of the beach, a tunnel allows access to some of the smaller bays.

Building density diminishes travelling westwards from here to the next resort, **Vau**. This offers a more relaxing atmosphere than Praia da Rocha and still has a very fine beach overlooked by a well placed café/restaurant.

Further on still lies the picturesque hilltop village of **Alvor** overlooking a river of the same name. It has a long historical connection, possibly founded by Hannibal, the great Carthaginian general, and may have been the original Portus Hannibalis since the river would have been more navigable in those days. It is a delightful village to explore, full of interesting cameos with its clustered houses jostling for a place on the narrow sloping streets. It had a castle once but the earthquake of 1755 demolished that so the best place to start an exploration is at the yellow and white parish church at the top of the village. This was rebuilt in the eighteenth century after the earthquake and has two very fine Manueline doorways, especially the one at main entrance.

One last port of call on this tour is **Ferragudo**, across the river from Portimão. Head inland to pick up the N125 and stay on the new road which by-passes Portimão to cross over the graceful suspension bridge. Leave by the first exit after the bridge towards Estombar and then follow signs to Portimão. Turn left before crossing the old bridge to head down into Ferragudo.

Ferragudo is an old fishing village sat on a hilltop overlooking the estuary of the River Arade. It remains an atmospheric jumble of hilly cobbled streets and narrow alleyways but its once dilapidated look is diminishing. Houses are being renovated and decorated bringing a new vibrancy to this still sleepy village. Just beyond the village lies the beautiful beach of Praia Grande with the castle of St John of Arade, now a private residence. The beach here is protected from the worst of the Atlantic breakers by a mole to the south, which makes it one of the finest beaches in Algarve for windsurfing.

Praia da Rocha

CAR TOUR 3:
THE GARDEN OF ALGARVE

The fertile limestone region covering the central part of the region, known as the Barrocal, is the timeless heart of old Algarve. Towns and villages here are little touched by tourism and are the real custodians of Algarve's culture. This day long tour intrudes on a number of these villages, large and small, allowing one to appreciate the slower pace of life and the unchanging routines of agricultural Algarve. Locals always say there are two Algarves, one south of the N125 dedicated to tourism and one north of this road belonging to the people, where fewer tourists bother to set foot. This is exactly where this tour heads.

Alte folk festival

Many villages will inevitably escape the net. The intention is to select a few of the more interesting places which may tempt visitors to return again to search out others for themselves. The chosen starting place is Estói, just north of Faro, and the finishing place is Paderne, just north of Albufeira.

Travelling either from the east or west, **Estói** is easily reached along the IP1 motorway by taking exit number five. If there is a chance to visit on the second Sunday of the month, take it. This is market day and Estói hosts the biggest and the best market in Algarve.

Another treasure awaits in Estói in the form of a Baroque palace. Only the gardens are open to the public with the palace visible through locked gates but there is still much unusual ornamentation to see including a replica statue of the three graces, suspected by some to be an original Canova. The iron gates just to the north of Estói centre mark the entrance to the gardens. A palm studded avenue leads towards the palace, once the home of the Carcaval family.

Built in the eighteenth century, it is a fantasy creation of architectural styles involving Baroque, Rococo and Neoclassic. There is plenty of opportunity to see examples of this on the terrace in front of the house. Here, a voluptuous marble lady drapes herself around a polychrome *azulejos* fountain, a theme mirrored on the other side of an assembly of yet more marble ladies. Sweeping balustrades lead down either side to the lower garden and a chapel guarded by a grill to protect the statue of the three graces watched over by Venus and Diana. Blue and white *azulejos* panels decorating the stairways maintain a racy theme of nymphs but there are busts of famous people, including the poet Milton, scattered around to keep a sober eye on things. For a look at the palace itself, climb the steps to the highest level and peer through the iron gates. Restoration of this building is well underway and it will be opening shortly as a *Pousada*.

Another of Estói's treasures is the remains of the Roman villa at Milreu

Estói market

I t is far more than a market, it is a country fair in the truest style. Be early to savour the bustling activity, the locals arriving from the country in pony and trap or on horseback, the activities in the show ring when the traditional high-wheeled carts of Algarve are in action, the farmers examining the livestock, breakfast cooking on the grill and the women fingering new dress material. This is the theatre of country life with all its customs and local atmosphere.

**Left: Estói Palace;
Azulejos Fountain**

**Below: Horse
drawn cart, Alte**

which lies on the right, a short distance out of the town, when heading east to pick up the São Brás road. An information leaflet is available, in English, which details the layout including the baths area. Here a small tub thought to be for the ladies is decorated in mosaic with a fish theme. There are other mosaics around but they are sometimes covered with sand for protection.

São Brás de Alportel, normally shortened to São Brás, is the next port of call and quickly reached from Estói. São Brás is a fairly large rural town which will not demand too much time but, if there is time for refreshments, try the almond cakes which are a local specialty. The town does have an interesting folklore museum, housed in an old mansion and displaying farming equipment, traditional costumes and household bits and pieces.

Loulé is the next stop. It claims to be the largest inland village in Algarve and is famous for handicrafts. In earlier times it was occupied by both the Romans and the Moors who left behind a castle which was rebuilt in the thirteenth century. Now only a few remnants of the walls remain but one of these provides a good setting for the tourist office in Rua Paio Peres Correia. Next to the office is a new museum, which sets out to display a traditional kitchen complete with pots and pans. In the same street as the tourist office is the small church of Nossa Senhora da Conceição. Its plain exterior is in total contrast to the interior. Brown doors open into a tiny chapel filled with blue and white *azulejos* tiles depicting scenes from the bible and containing a heavily carved and gilded altarpiece.

The craftsmen of Loulé

To see the craftsmen at work, wander around the narrow cobbled streets in the old heart of the town. Here, in dimly lit workshops, the artisans craft away making articles in leather, copper, wood, cane and assorted other materials and their produce is up for sale.

Loulé has a Moorish style municipal market which is busy most mornings but Saturday especially. On this day, the locals bring in their produce and the market spills into the surrounding streets. It has become something of a tourist attraction these days so it pays to be early before the coaches start to arrive.

Leave Loulé by heading into the northern countryside on the N396 leading to **Querença.** Turn left to enter this peaceful village and head straight for the village square. There is nothing to do here but sit at one of the shaded tables with the locals, enjoy the ambience and watch the world go by very, very slowly. Should lunch be calling, the Restaurant Bar de Querença here in the square has a fine reputation for the quality of its food which draws people in for miles around in the evenings.

For the onward journey to **Salir,** leave Querença back to the N396 and continue heading north. Shortly, the road sweeps around to head west and provides good views of a varied landscape. Salir sits on a summit off the main road to the left, follow the signs but be prepared to abandon the car somewhere below the village and continue through its narrow streets on foot. Head for the main square occupying a prime position on the summit with quite spectacular views over the northern serras. Salir was once a Moorish stronghold complete with castle but little of this now remains although relentless explorers will find parts of the wall to the west of the square.

Return to the main road and continue on to the next destination, **Alte**. This is a village that the tourists have discovered but not yet in a big way. It is a village of fountains with special appeal to the Portuguese themselves.

The fountains of Alte

Starting in the area of the fountains, the first encountered is Fonte de Bicas which is backed by an attractive blue and white *azulejos* panel depicting a monk and a girl at the well. Following the road up the riverside leads to Fonte Grande, which has a number of springs and where a mill has been converted into a restaurant. Full of picnic tables, wall seats and leafy shade, this area is especially popular with the Portuguese who have raised the humble picnic to unsuspected heights of feasting. This is also where crowds gather when there is a festival in full swing for the final flurry of singing and dancing which brings the event to a close.

To the west lies the village itself where narrow, cobbled streets squeeze between trim, flower-decked, whitewashed houses and where one or two cafés and handicraft shops lie in wait, out to catch trade from passing tourists. Modern market stalls by the roadside are where fish and fresh produce are sold. Alte may be a good way from the sea but fish is still highly prized and a large part of the diet.

Before the tour concludes head south from Alte, either along country roads via Monte Brito or along the main N270 for **Paderne** to see the old Moorish castle set out in the countryside. Watch out for the sign to the castle on the west side of town. Follow along this narrow road for a short way and park in the area of the fountain, which means about a 30-minute walk, or carefully drive the stable track which leads to the castle.

Now in ruins, Paderne castle occupies a romantic position on top of a hill protected on three sides by the River Quarteira. It was built in the time of the Moors but captured in 1249 when Dom Afonso III recovered Algarve for the Christians. Now only the outer walls remain and part of a chapel dedicated to Our Lady of Ascension. The presence of the chapel suggests that the castle was restored and remained in use for several centuries after its capture. From the chapel side, the castle looks down over a medieval arched bridge built on Roman foundations. Like other rivers in the region, it was once navigable until the process of silting up restricted access.

A municipal market selling local produce is found in most large towns, like Albufeira, Tavira, Silves, Portimão, Lagoa, Lagos and Vila Real. These are normally open weekday mornings. Many towns also have a market where traders move in to set up stalls for the day and where a much wider range of goods is on sale than fruit and vegetables. Those close to areas of tourism have adapted a little to include goods more interesting to visitors. Away in the smaller towns, it is an occasion of great excitement bringing the locals together to meet and chatter, maybe have lunch but for them it is an opportunity to buy clothes, cheese and ham, household goods and perhaps a rabbit or a hen.

Some of the bigger markets traditionally include animals such as horses, cows and goats and these, particularly Estói, have developed into country fairs full of the smells of cooking bacon, the tinkling of beer glasses and the sound of cow bells. Bargains are struck, deals are made in the temporary bars and eating places while the women ponder over dishes of olives, select cured hams and sausages or buy up the week's fruit and vegetables. It is a bustling atmosphere alive with interest and where diehard habits and customs of country folk can be observed, which might sometimes surprise and sometimes even shock.

Conveniently, the markets follow a regular timetable and some of the important ones are listed below.

Weekly: Saturday: Loulé, São Bras de Alportal
               Wednesday: Quarteira

Fortnightly: Albufeira, 1st and 3rd Tuesdays in the month
                 Armação de Pêra 1st and
                 3rd Thursday

Estói Market

Monthly: 1st Sunday: Almancil,
               Moncarapacho
               1st Monday: Portimão
               1st Friday: Sagres
               1st Saturday: Lagos, Paderne
               2nd Sunday: Estói, Lagoa
               2nd Monday; Algoz
               2nd Friday: Monchique
               3rd Monday: Silves
               3rd Thursday: Alte
               4th Monday: Messines
               4th Saturday: Tunes

CAR TOUR 4:
A TASTE OF ALENTEJO

H istoric Mértola, one of the most fascinating walled towns in Portugal, lies close by in adjoining Alentejo. It is just a stone's throw away from Algarve taking about one hour by car from Vila Real and two hours from Albufeira, offering glimpses of the extraordinary Alentejana landscape along the way.

Mértola, walled town

Beautifully situated alongside the Guadiana river, **Mértola** is unique in having significant remains of an old Roman port but the echoes of history reverberate through later times and both the Visigoths and Moors left their imprints. Too isolated to attract mainstream tourism, the pace of life is slow and the ambience within the old walled town an experience in itself. There is a castle to explore, some excavations to wonder over and some small but expertly presented museums rich in artefacts from the town. The best advice is to make an early start, allow plenty of time and make a full day of it. There is no worry about lunch as there are a number of excellent Portuguese restaurants around serving typical Alentejana food. Avoid Monday as museums are usually closed.

This tour assumes a starting point of Albufeira and describes a route which heads first up the IP1 towards Lisbon and cuts across country through Almodôvar and on to Mértola. The return route follows the line of the Guadiana river back to Algarve and picks up the IP1 again to return to central Algarve. Visitors staying at the eastern end of Algarve, at Monte Gordo, will find it quicker to follow the N122 northwards along the Guadiana river and return the same way.

Although the IP1 heading northwards from Albufeira is regarded as motorway, do not expect motorway quality roads for, once underway, the road rapidly reduces to single carriageway. (A new motorway is planned.) Green cloaked mountains provide the early scenery where crooked cork oaks make striking patterns when caught in the rays of the rising sun. Check the distance on reaching Santana da Serra and 1 mile (1.6km) later, just about at the top of the hill, turn right into a narrow surfaced road following signs to Almodôvar. Prepare to turn right again very shortly and then relax from route finding to enjoy fine views of some of Alentejo's varied scenery. Rolling wheat fields one

Scorching heat

Be warned, Alentejo suffers much higher temperatures in the height of summer than Algarve, frequently reaching and topping 40°C.

moment and flat topped holm oaks shading black pigs the next, all lie under a big blue sky.

Just beyond Gomes Aires there is the possibility of a short diversion into Santa Clara a Nova to see the folk museum. This houses a fascinating collection from farm tools to household furnishings and has an extension specially built to display artefacts from a nearby Moorish castle.

Almodôvar is unexpectedly large but signs guide the way clearly through the tortuous streets, around the main square and out onto the Mértola road. A further 6.25miles (10km) beyond Almodôvar is the chance of another side trip, this time to see a working windmill at **São Miguel de Pinheiro**. Old ovens nearby have been faithfully restored and are now used to bake and sell bread from flour ground in the windmill. Another good reason to stop here is to enjoy refreshments at the village café/restaurant, Maria e Antonio.

Eucalyptus trees shade the onward route and there are still more views of Alentejo's tree dotted plains, which look at their most enticing when painted in the green of springtime. There is no hint of Mértola until quite suddenly, after emerging from a fold, the impregnable walls of the old town spring unexpectedly into vision.

Mértola occupies a classic position on top of an easily defended hill and close to a navigable river, as it was in early times rather like Silves. They both have a castle but here comparison ends for Mértola is still largely enclosed within its walls and so much more compact.

History of Mértola

Known as Myrtilis, it held a key position for five centuries under the Romans, as a riverside port convenient for exporting mineral ores mined from the nearby deposits at São Domingos and agricultural products from the vast farms developed around Pax Julia (Beja). All this attracted people of power and wealth to settle here. Little changed with the arrival of the Visigoths and the town continued to prosper as it did under Islamic domination.

Known as Martula under the Moors, the town was twice capital of the region that included Beja. The Christian reconquest effectively brought the town's prosperity to an end when the shipping trade was transferred to Setúbal and Lisbon. There was another brief period of prosperity when a trade in shipping cereals to North Africa built up but there were difficulties with silting along the river, which eventually closed the port. Mining at nearby São Domingos continued as a viable trade through the first half of the twentieth century but this closed in 1968 effectively reducing Mértola to insignificance. Its historic past may well yet prove the key to its future since the town is setting out to preserve its historical relics with great sensitivity.

Perhaps the best place to start is the tourist office in the middle of town. The museums do not yet attract enough visitors to have them permanently staffed and open all year but they are keen to show them off to visitors and will readily open them on request. Leaving the tourist office, head for the castle in the old part of town. This leads very shortly past the small Museum of Islamic Art, although there are plans afoot to move it into new premises. On show here is the finest exhibition of Islamic pottery to be found anywhere in the country including some early examples of polychrome glazing.

Continuing uphill towards the castle, the route passes the white parish church which was converted from a 12th century Moorish mosque. Telltale signs are the square shape of the building, the horseshoe-shaped door at the rear and the prayer niche facing east (the *mirhab*), in front of which is now the main altar. Inside, the attractive rib vaulted roof, supported by columns that have incorporated some Roman capitals, was constructed after damage inflicted by an earthquake in 1532 which destroyed the minaret.

Opposite page: Piers of the old Roman port, Mértola

Mértola castle

Crowning the hill is the castle, now extensively restored. There is a lot of Roman stone incorporated still in the castle, which tells of its early origins but it was just as important to the Moors. After its capture for the Christians by the Knights of Santiago in the thirteenth century, restoration and strengthening work included building the keep. That indefatigable castle-builder, Dom Dinis (1279-1325) was along shortly afterwards to add further improvements and enlarge the town walls. A climb up to the top of the keep is worth it for the views over the town and the surrounding countryside. Also in the keep is a small museum displaying some Visigothic remains and outside, in the middle of the garrison courtyard, is a barrel-vaulted water system which is still in good condition.

Below the castle, to the north, is an area of excavations which was started in 1978 and has so far revealed a layer of Moorish artefacts with Roman remains below. Originally, this area was a Roman forum with a huge chamber, a *crypto-porticus*, forming the north wall. It took archaeologists five years of painstaking work to empty this 98ft (30m) chamber which produced a valuable collection of artefacts now housed in museums. The patios and kitchens of the Moorish houses built over the Roman remains are clearly evident in parts. Ask at the tourist office about access.

Leave the castle and wander down to the riverside to find the eigh-teenth-century clock tower complete with stork's nest. Near here is the Roman museum, which is located beneath the town hall. It was born out of one of those twists of fate that sometimes happen. Clearance of the site after the town hall had been destroyed by fire revealed the foundations of an early Roman villa. This was carefully excavated and preserved and the town hall was then rebuilt above it. The result is a fascinating museum housed on the actual site of a Roman villa displaying some of the artefacts found there.

Walking south from the clock tower while still looking over to the river gives a good view of the old Roman port. Still remaining are the substantial brick piers of the Torre de Rio, the river tower, built by the Romans to defend the port. A passageway leads down the middle of the piers to the riverside whilst the open arches protected the structure from flood damage. Above the arches was a pier patrolled and guarded by Roman soldiers.

Back in the square by the tourist office, beneath the market hall, is a small craft workshop to visit where local women are busy reviving old skills and spend their days weaving woollen goods by traditional methods. Heading north from the tourist office and staying ahead when the main road swings right, leads to the Museum Basilica Paleocrista. This Basilica was a sacred burial ground used first by the early Christians and later by the Moors. All the Moorish graves lie in an easterly orientation while the Christian graves have a different line. The large windows allow good views even when the museum is closed.

When lunch calls, there are two

good places to try; either Restaurant Avenida, on the roundabout, which has a selection of mainly pork dishes, including wild boar, at reasonable prices or Restaurant Alentejo, at Moreanes on the road to São Domingos, where the waiters wear traditional costume as a matter of course and where the food is equally traditional.

The alternative route back to Algarve follows the N122 south, passing close to Alcoutim, down to Castro Marim.

Right: Mértola, view from castle

Below: Mértola on Guadiana River

CAR TOUR 5:
ALONG THE GUADIANA RIVER.

An escape from the fast tempo of life along the coastline beckons those in search of pastoral tranquillity. Enjoy a flavour of the famous Pombaline architecture in the square at Vila Real de Santo António, or Vila Real for short, before heading upstream to Castro Marim, long an important frontier post with a castle and a fort. Pass through typical Algarvian hamlets, where old crafts are still practised, the river becoming a constant companion on the approach to the small whitewashed town of Alcoutim and its castle.

Vila Real

Start the trip in **Vila Real**, once a bustling ferry connection with Spain before the opening of the road bridge. Most prices here are shown in Spanish pesetas as well as escudos, to accommodate the Spaniards who flock across the ferry daily for bargain priced Portuguese textiles and even corks. Vila Real began life after the 1755 earthquake and its pleas-

ant square is at the heart of a grid system of roads, a plan devised by the Marquês de Pombal for the rebuilding of Lisbon's Baixo district. Pombal was the dictatorial prime minister at that time and planned Vila Real as an important port for fishing and trade further up river.

Orange trees add splashes of brightness and dappled shadows

darken the rays of the *calçada* paved square, which is surrounded by Pombaline style buildings, their roofs similar to those at Tavira. This is a good place to come for a coffee before ambling along the pedestrianised shopping streets or looking for bargains along the riverfront. Although the cost of a ferry trip across the river is minimal, except for curiosity value it is not really worth the effort but boat trips operate from Vila Real in summer as far as Alcoutim and sometimes even to Mértola.

Take the N122 north from Vila Real through the Sapal Nature Reserve to **Castro Marim**. The reserve is a great place for bird spotters (see Nature Reserves feature box).

History of Castro Marim

This goes back into the mists of time, even before the Phoenicians traded from there. It was heavily fortified once the Moors had been driven out of Portugal and became the headquarters of the Order of Christ, a new order founded after the Knights Templar was disbanded. Henry the Navigator was a Grand Master, but at the time when the Order's headquarters had been transferred to Tomar, and the white sails of his ships were emblazoned with the red cross of the Order. The castle was strengthened and the fort built in the seventeenth century after sixty years of Spanish domination.

Castro Marim's importance as a port declined after the 1755 earthquake and was hastened by the silting up of the river and a new port at Vila Real. Castro Marim is an even sleepier backwater since the main road was directed round the town. The castle and fort dominate adjoining hills from where there are sweeping panoramas.

Press on up the N122 towards Beja through Azinhal, noted for bobbin lace. Turn off right down towards the river, 4 miles (6km) past Azinhal, signposted to Alcoutim. The road now wends gradually downhill to reach the river at Foz do Odeleite where yachts bob gently at anchor. Life, like the river, moves at a slower pace here and villages such as Álamo, Guerreiros do Rio and Laranjeiras offer a glimpse into the past. Sanlúcar de Guadiana with its glowering Moorish fortress is often mistaken for Alcoutim on first sight but lies in Spain.

Alcoutim lies tucked around the next corner, its white, red-roofed houses clustered around the ruins of the castle. Old Alcoutim has retained its identity, a tributary of the river separating the old town from new development. Its history has followed a similar pattern to that of Castro Marim, albeit on a smaller scale, with service as a port and important strategic position. This was fine until hostilities between Spain and Portugal subsided and trade upriver decreased. The town reverted to being a quiet retreat where not much happened. No doubt to alleviate their boredom at this turn of events, the inhabitants appear to have been involved in the wholesale smuggling of tobacco and snuff during the seventeenth century.

The castle is the focal point of a visit, approached up a narrow cobbled street. Inside is a pleasant museum, which has been developed over excavations of Iron Age, Roman, Arabic and Medieval foundations. It is also worth the short climb up for the views from the castle ramparts. There are not too many choices of eating places here but there are cafés and the restaurant, O Soeiro, closed Sunday, shares a good riverside location close by the parish church. A ferry also crosses the river here to Sanlúcar.

From Alcoutim, either return the same way or alternatively drive uphill to rejoin the N122 and straight across into the N124 towards Cachopo and Barranco do Velho. This recently upgraded road is fairly straight as far as Martinlongo when it becomes more twisty. Look for the storks' nest on the church tower in Martinlongo. There has been a revitalisation of local craftwork in Martinlongo and at Cachopo, the next major village along the way.

The site of the **Cova dos Mouros** (Foupana Ecological Park) is easily reached via Cachopo from Tavira or as a diversion from this tour by turning south from the roundabout at Martinlongo. Head into the heart of inland Algarve, through unusual scenery, to observe 5000 years of history at these long abandoned ancient copper mines. They are now a museum where reconstructions of prehistoric houses and tools attempt to give some idea of life there at that time. Donkey rides are available for children and a Safari Park is currently being developed. There is a refreshment bar, lunch for pre-booked groups of 20 or more, and a minibus service from some of the main resorts (min 8 people).

There are a number of connections back down to the coast off the N124 but the road from Cachopo to Tavira is possibly the most scenic.

Countryside along the uadiana River with almond blossom in flower

Car Tours

Tour 1

Sagres fort
Open: 10am-8.30pm May-September and 10am-6.30pm October-April. Closed 1st May and 25th Dec.

Tour 3

Baroque Palace at Estói
The iron gates just to the north of Estói centre mark the entrance to the gardens.
Open 9am-12.30pm and 2-5.30pm. Closed Sunday, Monday and public holidays.

Roman villa at Milreu
Extensive site.
Open 9.30am-12.30pm and 2-5.30pm. Closed Monday and public holidays. Small charge.

São Brás folklore museum
61 Rua Dr José Dias Sancho.
Open 10am-1pm and 2-5pm Saturday and Sunday 2-5pm. Closed public holidays.

Tour 4

Mértola castle
The keep is open weekday mornings and afternoons. Closed Monday.

Museum Basilica Paleocrista
Tours of this museum are laid on at 11am and 3pm in season but it is best to enquire at the tourist office. Closed Monday.

Alte folk festival

Tour 5

Cova dos Mouros
(Foupana Ecological Park)
The site is signposted off left before reaching Vaqueiros.
Open daily (except in bad weather) 10.30am-6.30pm.
☎: 289 999229, fax: 289 999 436.

GETTING THERE.

BY AIR

Algarve, a major destination for the UK market, has an international airport at Faro. There are charter flights from all UK regional airports which are frequent in summer but less so in winter. There are also direct scheduled flights several times a week from Gatwick and weekly from Manchester.

BY CAR.

It is perfectly feasible to travel by car from the UK to Algarve. Drivers must be at least 18 years old, have held a full driving licence for at least a year and have full insurance cover for driving in Europe.

Ferry services to the Iberian Peninsula run from Plymouth to Santander and from Southhampton to Bilbão, both these ports are in northern Spain. There is a wide choice of routes leading south and crossing into Portugal presents no problems since the borders are now fully open.

ACCOMMODATION.

Algarve has many thousands of tourist beds in a whole range of accommodation from hotels, aparthotels, villas, mansions and timeshare, mostly of a very good standard. Away from the main season it is not generally difficult to find suitable accommodation but, in summer, tour operators book up most of what is available, especially self-catering villas and apartments.

HOTELS

All hotels are subject to registration and official classification with prices on display at reception and in the rooms. The charge is normally per room and breakfast may or may not be included. Also check if there are any hidden extras in the charge. The system of classification is mind-boggling and incomprehensible to most. Basically, the star rating refers to the number of facilities on offer and standard of decoration but these can mask indifferent service.

Other types of hotel accommodation are variously classified as:

Pousadas, state run hotels sometimes located in historic buildings, of which there are two in Algarve at São Bras and Sagres (soon to be a third at Estói)

Estalagems and *Albergarias*, hotels described as inns, which are similar to each other but their more consistent standard in general makes them a better choice than many similar starred hotels.

Aparthotels, self-catering apartments with hotel facilities

Motels.

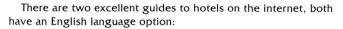

There are two excellent guides to hotels on the internet, both have an English language option:

www.maisturismo.pt

www.portugalinsite.pt

RESIDENCIALS AND PENSIONS.

A mixed bag of choices here as the hotel tag can seemingly be added at the whim of the owner. Both are actually similar but standards can vary enormously.

VILLAS AND APARTMENTS.

These make up by far the bulk of accommodation in Algarve and during the peak summer season are mainly occupied by clients of package tour companies. The majority offer a good standard of service and facilities for self-catering.

CAMPING.

Camping in areas other than on official camping grounds is not permitted but there are plenty of sites in Algarve. Information about *Parques de Campismo* can be obtained from the National Tourist Office or from the Regional Tourist Office of Algarve, Avenida 5 de Outubro, 18, 8000 Faro.

CAR HIRE.

Car hire is popular, especially for shorter periods of between three or four days in summer and longer periods outside the main holiday season. A current driving licence is all that is required for EU nationals, Americans, Canadians and Australians. The hirer must be over 21 and have held a full licence for at least a year. Driving into Spain with a hire car needs clearance from the hire company to ensure insurance cover, for which there may be an additional premium.

Portugal is one of the least expensive holiday destinations for car hire. With a little bit of research, a better deal can sometimes be arranged by booking and paying in advance of departure. Companies like Transhire (☎ 0870 789 8000 and Fax 01923 834 919) offer extremely competitive rates which include full insurance, collision damage waiver, unlimited mileage and various taxes, and use a leading Portuguese operator.

There is no shortage of hire companies in Algarve including the internationally known agencies. On the spot advertised car rates may sound enticing but check the details for the extras. Collision damage waiver (CDW) may not be included and it is imperative to take it. This cannot be stressed too strongly. Should you be unfortunate enough to be involved in an accident without CDW insurance and the costs cannot be recovered from a third party then the consequences can be frightening. At best you may be faced with a huge repair bill or detained until it is fully paid.

Tyres and damage to the underside of the car are mostly excluded from the insurance cover. Take time when accepting the car to inspect the tyres and, if not fully satisfied, do not accept the vehicle. It is worth a moment too to check that lights and indicators are fully operational. By law, cars should also carry a fire extinguisher, first aid kit and a warning triangle but hire cars usually only come with a warning triangle.

Make sure you have the agencies telephone contact number in case of breakdown.

MOTORCYCLES.

The above comments also apply to hiring a motorcycle or moped. Although the law clearly states that helmets must be worn, and the locals do now wear them, they are only available from some hire firms on request but you could be prosecuted for not wearing one. Check the tyres, brakes and lights before accepting a bike. Those intending to hire a motorcycle should check out the fine print in the medical section of the holiday insurance taken out in their own country. Such is the concern over motorcycle and moped accidents that some companies are specifically excluding injuries arising this way.

See also Driving in Algarve. (See page 100).

CHANGING MONEY.

Banks and money exchange facilities are plentiful in the main tourist areas. There is no problem exchanging bank notes or Travellers Cheques. Hotels offer exchange facilities but are not noted for generous rates.

Using cash machines, of which there are many throughout Algarve, is the easiest and cheapest way to obtain money. Provided your normal bank card, the same one which you use to withdraw cash from the machines at home, shows the *maestro* or *cirrus* sign then it can be used overseas with your normal pin number at ATM's displaying those symbols. Amounts up to £100 can normally be drawn daily although some machines state a higher maximum. There are also machines for changing notes.

Bank opening hours are Monday to Friday 8.30am-3pm or 8.30-11.45am and 1-2.45pm. Closed Saturday, Sunday and public holidays.

Faro airport bank is open from 8am-8pm but the post office 9am-7.30pm. Closed Saturday, Sunday and public holidays. ATM's are also available 24 hours.

CHEMISTS

Chemists (*Farmácia*) open 9am-1pm and 3-7pm Monday to Friday and 9am-1pm Saturdays. Duty chemists provide a 24 hour service, 7 days a week. Notices are displayed on the door of chemists' shops and in newspapers.

CLOTHING

Summer requires only light clothing with the addition of a few warmer items in spring and autumn. In winter, it can be jumpers one day and shorts the next, at least in the middle of the day, but it can be nippy early morning and in the evening.

Some items of clothing, especially shoes, can be had at bargain prices. The table below could be useful.

CLOTHES SIZS:

Men's Suits:

UK/US	36 38 40 42 44 46 48	
Portugal	46 48 50 52 54 56 58	

Dress Sizes:

UK	8 10 12 14 16 18
US	6 8 10 12 14 16
Portugal	34 36 38 40 42 44

Men's Shirts:

UK/US	14 14.5 15 15.5 16 16.5 17
Portugal	36 37 38 39/40 41 42 43

Men's Shoes:

UK	7 7.5 8.5 9.5 10.5 11
US	8 8.5 9.5 10.5 11.5 12
Portugal	41 42 43 44 45 46

Ladies' Shoes:

UK	4.5 5 5.5 6 6.5 7
US	6 6.5 7 7.5 8 8.5
Portugal	38 38 39 39 40 41

CONSULATES

Nearest foreign Embassies and Consulates are:

Canadian Embassy, Avenida da Liberdade, 144-156, 4th floor, 1200 Lisbon
☎ 21 347 4892

Canadian Consulate, Faro ☎ 289 880 880

UK Embassy, Rua S. Domingos á Lapa 37, 1200 Lisbon
☎ 21 396 1191

UK Consulate, Largo Francisco A Maurício, Portimão
☎ 282 417 800

USA Embassy, Avenida das Forças Armadas, 1600 Lisbon
☎ 21 726 6600

CURRENCY AND CREDIT CARDS.

The local currency is the *escudo*, abbreviated as esc. A written escudo sign comes after the whole number of escudos and is the same as the American dollar sign, 20$00. Figures after the sign are parts of an escudo or centavos, of which there are 100 in an escudo, but inflation has rendered these obsolete. Escudo notes commonly in circulation include 10,000, 5,000, 1,000 and 500 whilst escudo coins are in denominations of 200, 100, 50, 20, 10, 5, 2.50 and 1. The Portuguese usually refer to a thousand escudos as a *conto* or *contos* for multiples of a thousand.

Travellers Cheques and hard currencies are freely accepted at banks, Post Offices and Exchange Bureaux. Credit and charge cards are also widely accepted in hotels, shops and some restaurants. Do not count on paying for petrol with plastic cards although some of the larger stations will take them.

DRIVING IN ALGARVE.

Driving in Portugal is on the right hand side of the road with over-taking on the left. Give way to traffic from the right, which is not subject to a STOP sign. In the event of an accident where the driver was proven to be on the wrong side of the road, the insurance is invalidated.

Parking can be a problem in towns especially. Do not ignore parking restrictions, even if the locals do, illegal parking can result in a hefty fine. Pleading ignorance is not an accepted excuse.

Standards of driving are improving in Portugal, although the country has one of the worst accident records in Europe, but continue to be extra vigilant. Main roads are good but potholes, razor sharp edges and subsidence are still unexpected hazards to watch out for on lesser routes and road works may not always be properly signed.

A policy of zero tolerance operates in Algarve and driving regulations are fairly strictly enforced. There are on the spot fines, for which obtain a receipt.

Children under 13 must not travel in the front. Seat belts are compulsory in the front and also in the back, if fitted, at all times.

There are often spot roadside police checks so always carry your licence, passport and documents relating to the vehicle or face a heavy fine.

Drink-driving offences carry heavy penalties and the legal limit at 50mg is much less than in the UK (80mg). Offenders can face a heavy fine, withdrawal or suspension of their driving licence and/or imprisonment.

Petrol is freely available seven days a week in coastal areas but less reliable inland. Make sure the tank is full before making inland forays, especially at weekend and on public holidays. Grades of petrol (*gasolina*) are super = top grade petrol; *sem chumbo* = unleaded and *gasóleo* = diesel. Hire cars usually run on unleaded, which is freely available.

Speed limits are 75mph (120kmh) on motorways, 56mph (90kmh) on other roads and 37mph (60kmh) in built-up areas.

ACCIDENTS

Exchange insurance details if you are involved in a minor accident but the police must be called where injury and/or a more serious incident has occurred; in these circumstances do not move the vehicle before the police arrive.

BREAKDOWNS

It is a legal requirement to place a warning triangle 100yds/m behind the car. Next step is to contact the car hire agency or, if the car is private, contact the ACP breakdown service ☎ 21 942 5095. ACP has reciprocal arrangements with European motoring organisations, such as the British AA.

ELECTRICITY.

Mains electricity is supplied at 220/240 volts AC. Electrical equipment should be fitted with a continental two-pin plug or an appropriate adapter used.

EMERGENCY TELEPHONE NUMBER

112 (toll free).

FACILITIES FOR THE DISABLED.

There is a growing awareness of this problem and practical steps are being taken to improve matters. Most new building now makes allowances for access by the disabled as do some of the larger hotels. Ramps onto pavements or beaches are still few and far between or impossibly steep but at least the problem is slowly being addressed.

HEALTH CARE.

It is essential to take an E111, available free from Post Offices, in addition to travel insurance. Most private insurance companies top up the costs of any claim after E111 provision has been taken into account.

For minor ailments like headaches, mosquito bites or tummy upsets, head for the chemist shop (farmácia). Pharmacies are open during normal shop hours and most seem to speak some English. A rota of chemist shops provides a 24 hour service and the address of the duty pharmacist is displayed in the pharmacy window.

English speaking doctors advertise their services in the local English language newspapers and magazines.

Medical and dental treatment is available from health centres (Centro Medico). Show your passport, if a UK national, and ask to be treated under EU arrangements although a charge may be made. Between 20%-65%, or even the full cost, may be charged for prescribed medicines. State

dental treatment is very limited and the full cost usually payable. The same procedure applies for hospital treatment where there may be a charge for secondary examinations such as X-rays and laboratory tests.

LOST PROPERTY.

This should be reported within 24 hours to the police to obtain a report, which your insurance company will require.

MOSQUITOES.

Mosquitoes feed most actively at dusk and dawn but they can still be a nuisance throughout the evening and night. If you sit or dine outside in the evening cover up or use insect repellent. An electric machine in your room, which slowly vaporises a pellet, is very effective with the windows closed. *Anthisan* cream, especially applied immediately, is a calming treatment for bites.

POSTAL SERVICES

Post Offices (*correios*) open weekdays from 8.30am-6pm with smaller offices closing for lunch (12.30-2pm). Closed Saturday, Sunday and public holidays. Stamps (*selos*) can be purchased at the post office, sometimes at a special counter, from some shops displaying a '*correios*' sign, and from larger hotels when a small commission charge is added.

Although the postal system is reliable, if a speedy delivery is required ask for the express service, *Correios Azul* (Blue Post), which costs a little more. Post mail for this in the blue post boxes.

PUBLIC TOILETS

The most usual sign is WC with figures to indicate ladies (*senhoras*) or gents (*homens* and occasionally *senhores*). Larger towns like Faro and Albufeira have public toilets with an attendant, otherwise toilets can be found attached to markets and main rail and bus stations. If all else fails, it has been common practice to use the facilities of a bar or restaurant. Unfortunately, the sheer volume of tourists has led to many owners keeping toilets locked and only producing a key for customers. Either offer to pay for the service or buy a coffee or bottle of water. Toilet paper is usually supplied where there is an attendant and in most restaurants and occasionally elsewhere. Keep a supply with you.

PUBLIC TRANSPORT

Timetables are usually displayed at Turismo offices but copies can only be obtained from main bus and train stations, if demand has not exceeded supply.

BUSES

Paragem is the word for bus stop.

Express bus tickets and, with a few exceptions, tickets for buses from main bus stations are bought before boarding the bus. If in doubt, ask!

Good bus services, run by EVA, link all the main towns and villages along the coastal region of Algarve. This includes a daily express service between Lagos and Vila Real de Santo António and regular connections elsewhere. EVA also run connections to Sagres from Lagos, Faro to São Brás de Alportel, Faro to Loulé and a different company from Portimão via Lagoa to Silves. Besides these main connections there are other services to outlying villages but not necessarily every day.

During the summer season there are local buses to more inaccessible beach areas like Marinha near Benagil.

TAXIS

Black cars with a green roof make official taxis easily recognisable and be sure to use only official taxis. There are taxi ranks in all the main towns with radio cabs becoming more common. Most villages have a taxi, but they may be more difficult to pin down when needed. There should be a fixed rate from the airport to the various resorts so check this first. Metered fares apply at other times but it sometimes pays to ask around for a quote.

TRAINS

A railway runs the length of Algarve from Lagos to Vila Real de Santo António connecting with the line north to Lisbon at Tunes junction, close to the Albufeira station (*estação*).

The trains are relatively cheap and a number trundle along Algarve daily. Trundle being the operative word, the catch being the forty something stations along the way at which nearly all the trains stop. If getting there quickly is a priority opt for an express train, although it probably pays to check out the bus timetable first.

SHOPPING

Shops are open Monday to Friday 9am-1pm and 3-6pm or 7pm and Saturday 9am-1pm. The exceptions are the shopping malls and large supermarkets in Albufeira & Portimão which open 7 days a week until late and many shops in tourist areas, particularly during high season. Markets trade from Monday to Saturday between 8am and 1pm.

SPORTS & PASTIMES

Algarve is a great location for sporting activities of every kind. Some are listed below but head to the nearest tourist office for free literature with still more information. Look in particular for the free booklet *Algarve Tips*.

BOAT TRIPS.

Plenty of opportunities but particularly interesting are the trips around the Ria Formosa at Faro, the caves and grottoes in local fishing boats or sailing ship from Lagos and trips up the Arade river from Portimão or the Guadiana river from Vila Real.

FISHING

Organised fishing trips and equipment for hire in most resorts.

GOLF

Algarve is home to some of the finest golf courses in Europe hosting a full range of international competitions. The kind climate allows play all the year around with the greatest demand throughout winter and spring. In spite of the abundance of excellent courses, demand exceeds supply and the construction of new courses seems to be forever ongoing. A booklet giving course details is available from the tourist office.

HORSE-RIDING

Plenty of riding stables (*Centro Hipico*) in Algarve offering lessons for beginners, treks, beach rides etc: further information freely available from tourist offices and in tourist newspapers.

SAILING

Yachts and motor boats can be rented at the marina in Vilamoura, Faro, Lagos, Tavira & Vila Real but sailing is not for the inexperienced along the Algarve coast. Dinghies can also be hired at some tourist spots.

SCUBA-DIVING

Practised in the more rocky part of western Algarve. A number of diving companies offer courses, hire equipment and arrange trips.
    Atlantic Diving, Algoz ☎. 282 55 301 and other centres at Albufeira, Praia Senhora da Rocha and at Praia da Luz.

SNORKELLING

The rocky coastline to the west makes for more interesting snorkelling but watch the tides. A fierce undertow can make conditions unsafe in particular when the tide goes out. Special conditions and a licence apply for spearing fish.

SURFING

This is best along the west coast with its huge Atlantic rollers.

TENNIS

There are more than 20 tennis clubs throughout Algarve, some with floodlight facilities. Many offer individual and group coaching, clinics and tournaments.

WALKING

Algarve offers good opportunities for walking both inland and along coastal paths. See *Landscapes of Algarve* by the same authors, published by Sunflower Books.

WATER-SKIING

The best places to ski are in the quieter waters of the lagoon areas to the east and in the mouth of the Arade river at Ferragudo, opposite Portimão.

WINDSURFING

Schools which offer instruction and board hire are located all along the coast.

TELEPHONE SERVICES

Telephone calls from hotel or apartment rooms are usually fairly expensive.

Telephone boxes are operated by a crediphone card. Crediphone cards of usually 100 units are available from post offices and some shops and cafés that display the 'crediphone' sign.

It is also possible to make metered calls from some shops or cafés which display a CCT sign.

There are three area codes covering Algarve:

281 – Vila Real de Santo António to Tavira
289 – Olhão to Albufeira and
282 – Armação de Pera to Sagres.

The area code must be dialled at all times, even when telephoning numbers in the same area.

To telephone home, dial the country code but drop the first 0 in the home number.

International dialling codes from Portugal are:

UK & Northern Ireland	0044
United States & Canada	001
Australia	0061
New Zealand	0064.

TIME

Portugal lies in the GMT zone which means that it is the same time as the UK. Clocks are advanced for one hour in summertime, from March to October, in line with all other EU countries.

TIPPING

A service charge is included in hotel and restaurant charges. Tip for good service in a restaurant, helpful taxi drivers and also porters and maids at your accommodation.

TOURIST OFFICES

NATIONAL:

Leaflets on Algarve and general information on Portugal are available before departure from the Portuguese National Tourist Office, addresses as follows:

UK: 22/25A Sackville Street, London W1X 1DE.
☎. 020 7494 1441

Canada: 60 Bloor Street West, Suite 1005, Toronto, Ontario M4W 3B8. ☎. 416 921 7376

USA: 590 Fifth Avenue, New York, NY 10036-4704. ☎. 212 354 4403/4/5/6/7/8

REGIONAL:

The regional office for Algarve is situated in Faro and there are plenty of tourism posts scattered throughout the area. All supply printed literature and information. Bus and train times are also posted but timetables are only available from main bus and train stations.

Regional Tourist Office for Algarve
Avenida 5 Outubro, 8000 Faro,
☎ 289 800 400, Fax 289 800 489

TOURISM POSTS

Albufeira (8200) Rua 5 de Outubro.
☎ 289 589 279

Alcoutim (8970) Praça da República. ☎ 281 546 179

Aljezur (8670) Largo do Mercado.
☎ 282 998 229

Armação de Pêra (8365) Avenida Marginal. ☎ 282 312 145

Carvoeira (8400 Lagoa) Lg da Praia do Carvoeira ☎ 282 357 728

Castro Marim (8950) Praça 1st de Maio, 2-4 ☎. 281 531 232

Faro (8000) Rua da Misericórdia, 8-12. ☎ 289 803 604

Lagos (8600) Rua Vasco de Gama,
☎ 282 763 031

Loulé (8100) Edifício do Castelo.
☎ 289 463 900

Monte Gordo (8900) Avenida Marginal. ☎. 281 544 495

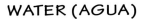

Portimão (8500) Avenida Zeca Afonso ☎ 282 419 131

Praia da Rocha (8500) Rua Tomás Cabreira. ☎ 282 419 132

Silves (8300) Rua 25 de Abril.
☎ 282 442 255

Tavira (8800) Rua da Galeria.
☎ 281 322 511

WATER (AGUA)

Algarve water is passed as safe to drink but can be loaded with chlorine and full of salts. Bottled water is the best option for drinking and there is quite a choice. *Agua mineral* comes either *com gas* (fizzy) or *sem gas* (still).

INDEX

LANDMARK
VISITORS GUIDES

US & British Virgin Islands

US & British VI*
ISBN: 1 901522 03 2
256pp,
UK £11.95 US $15.95

Antigua & Barbuda

Antigua & Barbuda*
ISBN: 1 901522 02 4
96pp,
UK £5.95 US $12.95

Bermuda

Bermuda*
ISBN: 1 901522 07 5
160pp,
UK £7.95 US $12.95

Barbados

Barbados*
ISBN: 1 901522 32 6
144pp,
UK £6.95 US $12.95

St Lucia

St Lucia*
ISBN: 1 901522 82 2
144pp,
UK £6.95 US $13.95

Pack 2 months into 2 weeks with your Landmark Visitors Guides

Jamaica

Jamaica*
ISBN: 1 901522 31 8
144pp
UK £6.95 US $12.95

Orlando & Central Florida

Orlando*
ISBN: 1 901522 22 9
256pp,
UK £9.95 US $15.95

Florida: Gulf Coast

Florida: Gulf Coast*
ISBN: 1 901522 01 6
160pp
UK £7.95 US $12.95

Florida: The Keys

Florida: The Keys*
ISBN: 1 901522 21 0
160pp,
UK £7.95 US $12.95

Dominican Republic

Dominican Republic*
ISBN: 1 901522 08 3
160pp,
UK £7.95 US $12.95

Gran Canaria

Gran Canaria*
ISBN: 1 901522 19 9
160pp
UK £7.95 US $12.95

Tenerife

Tenerife
ISBN: 1 901522 17 2
160pp,
UK £7.95

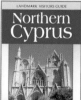

Northern Cyprus

North Cyprus
ISBN: 1 901522 51 2
192pp
UK £8.95

Madeira

Madeira
ISBN: 1 901522 42
192pp,
UK £8.95

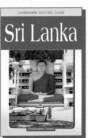

Published in the UK by
Landmark Publishing Ltd,
Waterloo House, 12 Compton, Ashbourne, Derbyshire DE6 1DA England
Tel: (01335) 347349 Fax: (01335) 347303
e-mail: sales@landmarkpublishing.co.uk
website: www.landmarkpublishing.co.uk

ISBN: 1 901522 92 X

British Library Cataloguing in Publication Data: a catalogue record for this book is
available from the British Library.

Print: Gutenberg Press Ltd, Malta
Design & Cartography: James Allsopp
Editor: Kay Coulson

Front cover: Olhos d'Água
Back cover, top: Festival at Alte, May Day
Back cover, bottom: Albufeira

Picture Credits:
All photographs are supplied by the author.

Acknowledgement:
Thank you to "hotter" (Tel 0800 468837) who supplied the authors with the
most comfortabe footwear they have ever worn; ideal for tramping around
Algarve while researching this book.

DISCLAIMER
While every care has been taken to ensure that the information in this book
is as accurate as possible at the time of publication, the publishers
and authors accept no responsibility for any loss, injury or
inconvenience sustained by anyone using this book.